Change One Belief

Inspirational Stories of How Changing One Belief Can Transform Your Life

Bob Burnham
Jeff McCallum
Rosemary Sneeringer
Kathryn Bartman

Change One Belief— Inspirational Stories of How Changing One Belief Can Transform Your Life

Copyright © 2012 by Bob Burnham, Jeff McCallum,
Rosemary Sneeringer and Kathryn Bartman
All Rights Reserved.

ISBN 13: 978-0-9848462-3-8
ISBN 10: 0984846239

Unauthorized duplication or distribution is strictly prohibited. The purpose of this book is to educate and entertain. The authors and/or publisher do not guarantee that anyone using these techniques, suggestions, tips ideas or strategies will meet with success. The authors and/or publisher shall have neither liability nor responsibility to anyone with respect to any loss or damage caused, or alleged to be caused, directly or indirectly by the information contained in this book.

Published by Expert Author Publishing
http://www.expertauthorpublishing.com

Canadian Address
1265 Charter Hill Drive
Coquitlam, BC V3E 1P1
Phone: (604) 941-3041
Fax: (604) 944-7993

US Address:
1300 Boblett Street
Unit A-218
Blaine, WA 98230
Phone: (866) 492-6623
Fax: (250) 493-6603

Table of Contents

What Others Say About This Book 7
Introduction 11
The Stories 15
Reunited—A Mother's Story of Adoption 16
Jeannie Trasolini
Manifesting Love From The Inside Out 20
Tammi Baliszewski, Ph.D.
The Gift of Peace 24
Kathy Kovacs
I Am More Than A Chicken Wing! 29
Davis Ehrler
Intuition and Mom Are Always Right 33
Vanna White
Right Under My Nose 37
Kay White
Change The End of Your Story 41
Johnell Borer McCauley
Willo's Story 45
Gabriella Taylor
Fishing Feels Better 49
Carter Peel
A Root Lesson 52
Rex Bohachewski

Gypsy Mermaid of the Rockies...............55
Marina Mermaid
Growing Up by Slimming Down..............59
Lorenzo Lamas
Our South African Awakening...............65
Brian Leslie
Driving Towards Joy...............69
Nancy Peet
Loving is a Choice...............73
Rebecca Skeele
When One Door Closes, Another One Opens...............77
Holly Eburne
No More Shame on You!...............81
Kit Furey, JD, CHt, CEHP
I Know This Much is True...............87
Rosemary Sneeringer
Always In Our Hearts...............92
Karin Volo
Leaping into the Unknown...............96
Shawna Craig
Shifting Gears...............101
J.F. Parkinson
Inspiration Versus Desperation...............106
Nikkea Devida
Stealing An Idea...............111
Anne Briggs Buzzini
'Til Death Do Us Part...............115
Amethyst Wyldfyre
Any Body Can Change The World!...............120
Ann Taylor

Meanings, Not Experiences, Create Our Reality 125
Irena O'Brien, Ph.D., ACMC
I Chose To Live 130
Kasia Rachfall
One Thought That Changed My Life Forever 134
Christine French
Buzz Kill 139
Kathryn Bartman
Taking Inspired Action and Investing in Myself 143
Lisa Sasevich
The Perfect Job 149
Bonnie Hope McDonald
The Big Guy with a Pink Feather Boa 153
Jen Cochran
Faith 157
Nicole Daga
Comedy of Terrors 161
Robert Calvert
Forgiveness Brings Freedom 166
Barbara Halcrow, MSW
A Transformational Turning Point 171
Eva Gregory, CPCC
Rif-sen, My Four-Legged Soul Mate 175
Romana Van Lissum
The Other Mother 180
Michele de Reus
True Financial Freedom 184
Bob Burnham
Love Unexpected 189
Monica Regan

The Tools *193*
Self-Soothing
Healing From the Inside Out *195*
Tammi Baliszewski, Ph. D.
How To Identify Your Subconscious Beliefs
in Minutes *202*
Nikkea B. Devida
A Tool to Achieve Instant Breakthroughs to Your Ideal
Results in Any Situation *223*
Kit Furey, JD, CHT, CEHP
Meta Belief Change Technique *244*
Irena O'Brien, Ph.D., ACMC
Information on Contributing Authors *256*

What Others Say About This Book

Don't let your beliefs stop you! Get *Change One Belief* now, believe in yourself, follow your heart, and live your dreams and start creating the life you were born to live.
—**Jim Donovan, author, *This is Your Life, Not a Dress Rehearsal***

Change One Belief is an impressive collection of diverse and inspiring stories. Most importantly, it's a book about transformation, a power each and every one of us possesses to make dynamic changes in our lives…A very fulfilling read!
—**Mark Angelo, renowned river advocate, speaker, writer and educator, World Rivers Day Founder and Chair**

We're born with a clean slate, free and clear of limiting beliefs. As we grow, we begin to adopt beliefs, form them from our experiences and rarely stop to ask the question – is this belief true? Change One Belief shares true and poignant stories of people who have stopped to question their limiting beliefs. It's a wakeup call for everyone – a challenge to take a look at our own lives and ask the difficult and freeing questions.
—**Annette Elton, Author**

Congratulations on this innovative project. Readers can't help but be inspired to make changes in their own lives from the wealth of examples that they find in the stories contained in Change one Belief. Having seen such work first hand, I certainly was.
—**John E. Earhart, Chairman, Global Environment Fund**

This extraordinary book is life-changing. It shows you how to unlock more of your true potential than you ever thought possible.
—Brian Tracy, Author, Change Your Thinking, Change Your Life

Introduction

For hundreds of thousands of years we have learned through stories—etched out on cave walls, shared at mealtimes, written in books or pictured in movies. By telling tales of triumph through adversity, we imprint hope on the new chapters in our own lives.

When we read or hear a compelling story we remember it and often pass it on to others. It's easier to remember new information when there's an interesting narrative around it. Effective teachers are more than instructors, they're also good storytellers, and true-life tales are the most gripping.

The idea for *Change One Belief* came to me at 2:00 a.m. after waking from a deep sleep. I ignored it at first, but it was persistent. By the fourth time the idea returned, I knew it was a book I had to do. Real life stories are the best way to illustrate how powerful a belief change can be because everyone can relate. These stories deliver on the promise of discovery and transformation that we all crave in our entertainment.

Beliefs are the operating system of our lives. If we have limiting beliefs, we will have a limited life experience.

Change our beliefs and we can be, do or have anything we want.

Look at any baby born and you see a loving, abundant and blissful little human. Some of us spend our lives trying to get back to this state after parents, teachers, the media and countless other factors form our beliefs for us. Although every situation holds infinite possibilities, most people have learned to see only a very small portion of them.

Our caretakers as we grow up do the absolute best they can with the information they have and the upbringing they experienced. Unfortunately, very few people break out of these patterns during their lifetimes. Usually, people live much the same lives as their parents did, and they pass on similar belief systems to the next generation.

Beliefs are thoughts we think over and over again until they become truths. The problem is we don't realize these truths are just thoughts that can be changed. If you have a belief that doesn't serve your best interest, you can change it. By changing a single belief, in many cases, you can literally transform your life.

Where people struggle is trying to control the external elements (changing jobs, moving to a different town), failing to realize the only way to alter the external factors is by changing the internal situation—your belief system.

In my own life, changing a few key beliefs transformed my entire existence.

The main reason I wanted to publish this book is because we are all only one belief away from changing struggle to bliss, poverty to abundance and anger to love. I have been more aware of this because now I help others achieve their goals. What I've found is I can give my clients a roadmap, blueprint or step-by-step guide, but if they have a belief that stands in the way of what they truly want, then none of that will work for them.

We are the sum total of our thoughts and beliefs so we must make sure our thoughts and beliefs are creating the lives we want. There is no other way.

This book is meant to be a BIG BOLD LIGHT, showing how people have Changed One Belief and transformed their lives, becoming a beacon of light and a shining example for others.

This book has its own energy—that of a positive, abundant, loving and blissful world—and will influence anyone who reads it or even carries it. I encourage you to touch as many people as possible with this book by passing it on or buying copies for others.

If you think about it, we are all only One Belief Change away from a war-free world with no violence or One Belief Change away from abundance and bliss for all. This book reminds us that we can all be the light!

Blessings!

Bob Burnham

The Stories

Reunited—A Mother's Story of Adoption
Jeannie Trasolini

My husband and I paced up and down the hotel room, the time dragging by slowly by as we waited for him to arrive. Both of us had so many butterflies in our stomachs we could have levitated. How would he feel about us? Would we feel a connection? Would he be angry or resentful? What if he had piercings, tattoos or, heaven forbid, a mohawk!!!?

The much-anticipated knock finally came on the door; we were going to meet the son we had given up for adoption 24 years ago.

We eagerly opened the door and the first words out of my mouth were "Oh my God, you look like me!" We hugged each other and I felt as if I had always known him. I was excited, thrilled, over the moon. It was a huge roller coaster of emotions. It seemed impossible that here we were, after all those years, looking into the face of our grown-up baby boy—we wanted to pinch ourselves. It was joyous; it was momentous. It was a miracle.

Of course he had questions for us. What were the circumstances and how were we feeling when we gave him up for adoption? We answered his questions and I told him, "I was a child having a child," and he understood. We explained that we didn't know that three years later we would be married.

With all of us talking a mile a minute, he told us his story. After adopting him, his parents went on to have two daughters of their own. The following week we met and bonded with his entire family, sharing holiday celebrations and even taking a cruise together

Back in the sixties, when our son was born, there was a tremendous amount of shame for girls who found themselves in "the family way," and there were many young teenage girls who would disappear for several months supposedly visiting relatives or any other myriad reasons to explain their absence.

My boyfriend felt guilty and sad because I was sent to a home for unwed mothers, but he was incredibly supportive; even so I felt lonely, abandoned—and that my mother was right, I was bad to the bone.

Because of her constant criticism and judgment, I had grown up believing that I was worthless and now, pregnant at 15, I had proved just how unworthy I really was.

Keeping the secret of our son meant that we had to live a lie. Shame is a terrible burden. How can you be who you are when there is a large part of you that no one knows about? I was terribly afraid that if anyone found out my secret I would be diminished in their eyes. No one knew about him for twenty-four years.

But as our sons grew older—they were now 19 and 15—we started to talk about the possibility of finding the one that was missing. We had never talked about our son, I guess if we did it would make him real, and we would have to deal with the enormity of what we had done. This was something I hadn't really understood until I became the parent of two more sons and realized how much I loved my children and how important they were in my life.

When we made the decision to find him, we were determined that we would no longer be controlled by our shameful secret. We had changed our belief about reuniting with our son and now we felt that if anyone had a problem with it, it would be their issue, not ours.

All of my life I had lived in the dark, suffocating and soul-destroying shadow of shame and I was determined that from now on, no matter what it took, I would somehow find the courage to speak about him.

I remember many times I would have a huge knot of fear in my belly and be absolutely dying inside as I forced myself to speak about him, but I had made a vow and I could not and I would not go back to the way I used to be. My mantra became, "Feel the fear and do it anyway."

I became a catalyst for others to find the courage to look for their own lost children.

One summer, sitting around a campfire, I began to tell our story, and as I did, a woman across the campfire became visibly upset. Afterwards she came to talk to me and I said, "You've given up a child haven't you?" She answered, "Yes, I did, and because of you I'm going to tell everybody." Since she had been crying so openly I replied, "Honey, I think they already know." But even as she spoke I could see that her shame was so deeply ingrained in her, I doubt that she ever looked for the child that she was so heartbroken about.

Each and every time I told my story, people were amazed, thrilled and genuinely happy for me. No one judged me! In fact, I became a catalyst for others to find the courage to look for their own lost children, and in one instance I inspired someone to introduce his eleven-year-old, out-of-wedlock son to his family.

Confronting the shame and standing up for myself was my first major step in becoming the person I was meant to be. The young me was so sensitive about how people would look at me or what they would say about me. I was a people pleaser, hypersensitive because of my abusive childhood. And my shameful secret only reinforced the message I had heard over and over growing up: that I was worthless.

Once I accepted myself, I became self-confident and aware. I was born a people person. Growing up, I tried to get people to like me. Now I had come back to who I was meant to be. I don't let others define me anymore. I know who I am.

Shame is a terrible burden, it forces you to live a lie, to hide yourself from even your closest friends. I am happy to say I haven't felt shame in a very long time. I have come full circle.

My son is part of my life and lives close by with this wife and two daughters—interestingly, in the same exact place that he spent the first month of his life while waiting for his adoptive family.

To learn more about Jeannie Trasolini, visit www.expertauthorpublishing.com/cob.

Manifesting Love From The Inside Out
Tammi Baliszewski, Ph.D.

I was in shock, trembling as I listened to the "Entertainment Tonight" interview. The familiar laugh rang in my ears; the well-known baritone voice of my on-again, off-again fiancé sharing ecstatic details about the love of his life...and realizing he wasn't talking about me.

I had been with him for three years, through the ups and downs of award shows, substance abuse, addiction, love, lust and lies. He had just gotten out of rehab, and I felt confident we were going to work it out—because he told me we would. But somewhere on the way to Happily Ever After, my fairytale went horribly off-track and became a full-fledged nightmare.

Dizzy with confusion, I picked up the phone to speak to my fiancé, my priest, our therapist, and my friends. Each found an excuse not to talk to me. I had given up my career, distanced myself from family, from friends, and from God. This relationship had been my whole life and, just like that, without explanation, I was cut off and thrown away. I felt utterly devastated and alone.

Stumbling into the bathroom, I caught my reflection in the mirror. A gaunt stranger with dark circles under her eyes, and a puffy, tear-streaked face stared back at me.

"I want to go home," she whispered. In that instant I felt suicide was the only answer. I deserved to die for what I had done with my life. Anguish and despair brought me to my knees. I couldn't breathe, I was suffocating.

"God, help me!" I gasped. Everything went dark as I lost consciousness. Floating between dimensions, I felt as if I was being comforted in the unconditionally loving arms of my grandmother. For a moment I was safe, supported, and adored. Emerging from the darkness, I experienced an eerie reassurance that my path would be made clear before me.

Revelations dropped into my awareness as I basked in the warmth of a love that radiated from somewhere inside myself. I did not want to die, but I wanted to die to this old way of being. So what if this one man did not love me? What if I really was loved, safe and supported by God and the Universe? Perhaps what was happening was really bigger than my small story. It occurred to me if I could get through this, someday, I would be able to guide others through dark terrain and out of the depths of their own despair.

I rose, trembling like a newborn foal. Still shaking, I steadied myself against the wall and emerged from the bathroom. Despite the uncertainty of my life, a spark of optimism and hope had been ignited. I realized God was more powerful than my fiancé or any man, and I knew something important had shifted. Rather than needing to be validated by a man's acceptance, my priority was my relationship with Spirit, my healing path, and myself. I would devote myself to love, healing, and wholeness, so that I could help others one day.

***Instead of telling God what I wanted, I asked
God what He wanted of me.***

My past few years had been filled with concerns about what to wear and what people thought of me. Now my concern was learning to love myself and love others. I prayed in earnest and asked God for signs for the direction He would have me go. Instead of telling God what I wanted, I asked God what He wanted of me.

The next day I ventured outside of my apartment and sat in the sunshine, wondering what was to come. In a few minutes, a neighbor sat down beside me. She began to tell me about a school that focused on the body/mind/Spirit connection. It was clear this was the direction I was being invited to explore.

As I walked through the heavy glass doors of the Institute of Psychostructural Balancing, I knew I was home. I signed up immediately and immersed myself in school. I studied massage therapy, cranial sacral, polarity balancing, and hypnotherapy. Within weeks, I went from a life of luxury, limousines, and personal shoppers, to homework and dragging around a heavy massage table—my ego was shattered, and my soul celebrated.

I found I enjoyed the learning process and was a very good student. As I studied, my appetite to know more increased. I ventured into the realms of psychology, spiritual psychology and metaphysics. Relaxing into my confidence, I knew I was ready to be of service. I volunteered for hospice, and began to work with women in prison. Years passed. The people I connected with told me I gave them hope. The sentiments I received from friends, clients, and students were reminiscent of the encouraging message that had dropped into my awareness years ago on the bathroom floor.

Not so long ago I believed being abandoned and betrayed by my celebrity fiancé was the very worst thing that could have happened to me. I had lived at the pinnacle of an ego-based life, a life of materialism, fear, disconnection, self-loathing and sadness. I had attempted to live from the outside in, seeking from material things a sense of value, love, and fulfillment. In fact, that "worst thing" was the opening of a door into a larger, more loving and more authentic life. Fourteen years after my breakdown, I am a counselor, the author of *Manifesting Love From the Inside Out,* the host of a radio show on Empower Radio, a sacred art facilitator, and the CEO of a non-profit organization. I am also very happily married to an incredible man.

My breakdown was really a breakthrough, and supported me in the understanding that the Kingdom of Heaven is within. A Zen teaching says, "Heaven and hell are 1/10 of an inch apart." In those moments on my bathroom floor I broke through hell to the place of love that resides within myself—and I committed to let that love be my guiding light for the rest of my life.

To learn more about Dr. Baliszewski, visit
www.expertauthorpublishing.com/cob.

The Gift of Peace
Kathy Kovacs

*Not being seen or heard for who you really are
is one of the most painful things a human can endure.*

The sound of the doorbell wouldn't stop. I remember wishing it was my alarm clock going off. That would've been easier. Just reach over and hit snooze. Or throw it against the wall. I slowly sat up, blinking my tired eyes to help get focused.

Then it hit me.

The ringing sound had nothing to do with an alarm clock or a doorbell. Those are familiar sounds you hear at home. That was the problem. I wasn't at home. I was IN a home. Never before had a preposition literally become a defining point in my life.

The beeping sound was the IV drip in my arm. It had run dry and the nurses would need to change it soon. It was Day Four for me and routine had finally set in.

I would spend a total of 14 days of my life in a home for abused women during the winter of 2005. I was eight and a half months pregnant at the time.

I remember feeling ashamed and embarrassed that life had led me here. How did this happen? "I'm a successful career woman with a university degree. I make a good salary with a big company in a high-profile position. I'm a mom, a step-mom, and a soon-to-be mom. *How did I get here?"*

What I did as soon as I was out of there was just as alarming. I went back to him.

Over and over again.

Each time I would hold out hope that maybe this was finally the "rock bottom" everyone talks about and things would be different from now on.

Not so. As it turned out, the only constant in any of this would be the chaos.

My heart hurt and my soul ached as I exerted every ounce of energy I had into trying to be heard or understood. For the longest time I kept thinking, "If I could just improve my communication with him and get him to see how his words and behavior are harmful to me, then surely he would stop doing and saying those things. *Wouldn't he?*"

It became a cycle. Anger, silence, blaming then belittling—I was drowning in waves of emotion that rocked me to my core and eroded all sense of self-worth. Only a shell of who I once was remained. After a decade of this, I began contemplating that the easiest way out may very well be death.

Fortunately, I was always able to reach out and ask for help whenever personal desperation trumped rational thinking. There were also counselors, self-help books, and advice from community experts that certainly helped along the way. But, in the end, none of it was enough to weather the rage-filled storms and the substance-fueled tirades that found their way into so many of our days and nights.

At its very worst, I experienced angry hands grab at my neck and squeeze my throat as I was wrestled to the ground. There was fighting back...and then blacking out...I remember it happening once in our son's room as he lay asleep in his crib. Any mention of it the next day was either denied outright or forgotten altogether.

I would later come to realize that you don't live through this kind of pain. You survive it. It's a very private and complex kind of hurt which is compounded by the humiliation of experiencing it at the hands of a person who happens to be your *partner.*

It's not the kind of feeling that simply garners a warm hug or a quick wink of an eye to suggest we've all been there before and the hurting will soon pass. There are no get well cards for this kind of hurt nor are there bandages or casts to help heal wounds caused by verbal lashes or emotional attacks.

Solace came from unlikely places. One day I remember being in the grocery store and seeing an older woman—a stranger—look at me and simply smile, as if to say hello. I felt her warmth and it comforted me. *I'm still alive and I count,* I remember thinking. *She sees me as a person.* A small gesture though it may have been, it was moments like this that helped restore my sense of mindfulness. Strength began to rise in me and hope soon followed.

I started challenging him and for that I would pay the price—but it was so far gone by then, there was nothing left to lose. I had had enough. I remember that day well.

Little did I know it would be just hours before my life would change forever on that day in April of 2011.

***

Red and blue lights twisted through our dining room windows. One police officer stayed downstairs with him in the family room while the other one came upstairs and talked with me while I sat on the edge of my bed. My right arm was throbbing and beginning to swell. *I can't believe our sons slept through it all.* And for that I was so very grateful.

Grateful for that and for the fact it was finally over.

This is the stuff that alters one's direction in life and pushes one out of their comfort zone for the good of others.

On Thursday, February 23rd, 2012 at 10:31 am, I got a phone call from Victim Services telling me he was acquitted. My legs began to quiver and my heart started racing as I heard the news. I listened to the explanation the judge had given to those in attendance and how the judge admitted "something went on that night" but it was nothing that could be proven beyond a reasonable doubt. I asked if that meant all of the restraining orders, third party contacts, and bail conditions are now null and void. The lady from Victim Services confirmed that yes, that was now the case. I thanked her and hung up. I sat in silence listening to my heart pound and my mind race. Then, I looked around and noticed the bright sun streaming through my huge picture windows, my dog basking in the warmth, the comfortable feeling of my favorite rocking chair and the calmness surrounding my new home. I took a deep breath and shrugged. I now know how the system works and most importantly how it doesn't. The outcome did not surprise me. If anything, the not-guilty verdict will force me to challenge more of the court's procedures and push forward to help others navigate through this outdated, unrealistic, and biased system. It's been an empowering journey. This is the stuff that alters one's direction in life and pushes one out of their comfort zone for the good of others. I am up for the challenge. I'm smiling as I realize the insignificance of the judge's ruling. Somehow, the quest for victory, the desire to get revenge, and the struggle to simply win at all costs fell by the wayside a long time ago. Instead, I have received gifts of far greater consequence.

I know this because, for the first time since I can remember, my mind is settled, my heart is warm and my body feels relief. *I am at peace.*

To learn more about Kathy Kovacs, visit
www.expertauthorpublishing.com/cob.

I Am More Than A Chicken Wing!
Davis Ehrler

There they were, being placed in the middle of our table, a piping hot plate of bright-orange, promise-to-burn-your-mouth, chicken wings. As the perky waitress set the plate in front of me I watched the greasy sauce drip from a drumette onto the neatly arranged celery sticks. I thought to myself, "There could at least be a candle stuck in one of them." It was my birthday after all.

"I'm sorry. I know this isn't the birthday dinner you were expecting," my boyfriend of over three years Rob said to me with compassion but little action as he put the ice-cold mug of beer to his lips.

I melted deep into the place inside myself I thought might save me. I looked out the water-streaked window and allowed myself to be consumed by the pouring rain. Everything felt heavy and gray, the low dense clouds poured out their truth. I wanted to do the same. The dull ache residing in my chest was holding my anger and tears hostage. I did not know what to say, how to feel, or what to do. What I DID know was if I opened my mouth for anything other than stuffing a bleu cheese smothered wing in it—I might fall apart. I swallowed hard and forced the shame and loneliness down into a dark corner inside of myself.

What happened to me? Where did I go? I missed the woman who believed in herself and believed in love. I missed the woman who had a deep and abiding faith. If the tears were available I would cry for the woman who went from a bright, brilliant light to a silent, gray shadow; for the woman who stayed in a relationship that was riddled with red flags from the start; for the woman who stopped believing in herself to satisfy the insecurities of another; for the woman who had been slowly chip, chip, chipped away at and was now a shadow of her former self.

The cheer of the crowd watching the football game brought me back to reality. I adjusted my posture and took in the deepest breath my lungs would allow. The spice of my special birthday wings was clearing out my sinuses and apparently my soul. I could feel the truth attempting to break free inside of me.

I smiled weakly at Rob and reflected on the last few years. On my 39th birthday Rob asked me to marry him, and we made plans to be get married on my 40th. That didn't happen. My day had become less important each year. Every year I gained a bigger number but lost another piece of me.

Rob interrupted my thoughts, "Are you okay?" I nodded. "Yeah, I'm good," I heard myself say, a lie spicier than the wings. The truth—I was NOT good, in fact, I was pissed off. I wanted to yell out, "How could I *possibly* be good, *ya jack wagon*? IT'S MY BIRTHDAY!!! It is the fourth birthday we have spent together and THIS is what I get? You made no plans, no gift, no card, and we are eating happy-hour CHICKEN WINGS for my birthday celebration!"

But I didn't.

After our gourmet dinner of chicken wings, we drove back to my house. When we walked in, there was my gift—my journal, sitting open on the coffee table. Earlier that day I had written in large red letters: "I am ashamed of myself for still being with Rob." Rob's eyes rested on my journal for a moment and then looked at me. My heart sank. The truth was exposed for all to see. Once again, he showed me who he was and who I had become. With rage darkening his eyes, he told me I was a horrible human being and he was done with me. He walked out.

Happy Birthday to me!

I went to my bedroom and sat in the dark feeling alone and a bit relieved. I turned on the small lamp beside my bed and picked up a book I had been reading. I randomly opened to a page and there were the words my heart needed to hear, "No one can treat you worse than you treat yourself."

Goose bumps washed over me.

The truth had arrived like a chorus of singing angels. Inwardly I heard the message, "You are MORE than a Chicken Wing! You DO Matter and you DESERVE the BEST."

A smile spread across my face as tears rolled down my cheeks.

I felt the dark cloud lifting, I was starting to understand the Universe had given me abundant opportunities to REMEMBER, BELIEVE and CLAIM that I do MATTER and that I DESERVE THE BEST for quite awhile. I just wasn't ready to hear it ... until I was ... over a plate of CHICKEN WINGS on my most favorite of days. Then I said out loud, "I AM READY!"

As I started to show up differently in the world, the world started showing up differently for me.

And would you believe as quickly as I became aware of that belief, changed it and claimed it, wonderful things started to happen? The next day a friend gifted me a nurturing day at the spa. My family was more generous than ever. Creativity started to flow. I started to take inspired action. My friend base naturally shifted as the most wonderful people began showing up in my life. It is shocking but not surprising as soon as I started to show up differently in the world, the world started showing up differently for me.

Beliefs are the compass to our existence. I now believe, and know, I can't change, fix or take responsibility for anyone other than me. My beliefs about me will lead the way. I now know I will always get what I believe. So why not believe the best of me?

Now I BELIEVE! I do MATTER! And I DESERVE the BEST!

And more importantly, I KNOW I AM MORE THAN A CHICKEN WING!

So are you ...

To learn more about Davis Ehrler, visit www.expertauthorpublishing.com/cob.

Intuition and Mom Are Always Right
Vanna White

Growing up in North Myrtle Beach, South Carolina, my mother always said to me, "Don't do anything you don't want to do. If that little voice in your head says, 'Don't do it,' listen to that little voice."

Years later, I drove out to Los Angeles to become a movie star. I got an agent, I was going on auditions, and I moved into my own apartment. One month I was strapped for money, and I was too embarrassed to ask my dad for $1000 for the rent. I wanted to prove I could make it on my own, so I posed for some lingerie shots.

I knew from the time I agreed to do them that it was the wrong thing to do. As the day of the photo shoot got closer, I felt a growing sense of dread. Posing for the pictures, I thought: This can't be good. But of course I'm also thinking: Oh, no one's ever going to see these!

Wrong. The whole world saw them!

I was photographed in the early 80s and I didn't get on "Wheel of Fortune" until November of '82. By '83 the show was getting quite popular. So of course, when I became famous, all of a sudden these old pictures surface, and they are sold to *Playboy*. They weren't nude but they were still revealing.

I spent several sleepless nights or woke up in the middle of the night worrying. The uncertainty and anxiety of the situation was making me sick to my stomach—I really thought my career was over! I'd get up to go to work and think: this could be my last time, my last week—I just didn't know what Merv Griffin's reaction would be.

But Hugh Hefner was a friend of mine. He was the first person I thought of to try to stop the photos from being published. I wasn't nervous about asking him at all, I really thought he would grant me this favor, friend to friend. But by the end of our talk, it became clear to me that he wasn't budging. I begged him, "Please do not put those pictures in your magazine," but he told me it was out of his control. I felt hurt, deceived and betrayed that a friend would take the chance of ruining my career. I did not trust him after that, and I stopped going to the Playboy Mansion.

I was so embarrassed. The thought of my friends and family seeing the pictures was sickening. As soon as I knew the pictures would go public, I called my family immediately. I didn't want the people I loved to be disappointed in me. I felt I was letting them down. So I braced myself for the worst.

But my family was so supportive. My dad said, "Honey, why didn't you just come to me? Don't ever do anything you don't want to do. You can come to me for anything."

When the issue hit the newsstands, I got out there, did publicity, and went on the talk shows to tell everyone the true story of what happened. I urged them to "Listen to that voice in your head! Don't do anything that doesn't feel right. Follow your instincts!"

Fortunately for me America didn't turn against me. They could have easily done that. I had just gotten

"Wheel" and I was up and coming, and then all of a sudden this "All-American Girl" appears on the cover of *Playboy*. It definitely could have been devastating, but it wasn't.

I regretted not listening to what my mother told me. The more I think about that, I feel how special that advice was, because so many people are outer-directed, with parents having an attitude of "What would the neighbors think?" So to have my mom emphasize what I consider not only your conscience, but using your own intuition as a guide, seems quite amazing to me now.

I've been offered a lot of money to shoot commercials that I've turned down. I will never put my name on something that I don't believe in, that I don't use myself, or that I don't feel is right in my heart. That's a belief that I was raised with.

If you stop for a minute and listen to that voice, it will guide you down the right road.

We make many choices in life, in our careers, in our personal lives, and it's so comforting to know that if you stop for a minute and listen to that voice, it will guide you down the right road. If you have a question, if you're unsure about something, all you have to do is listen or feel your way through it, because your body will tell you what's right too, whether your heart feels light or your stomach goes into knots of anxiety—the answer is right there.

Lots of times you might be saying, "Yes," and you're thinking, "No, no, no." "Yes," this way would be so easy, it would solve a lot of my problems—but you know it will probably cause a lot more problems in the long run! If we come up against a principle that's hard to learn or live by, we tend to take the easy way out instead of just listening to that voice. The people I know who follow their hearts are more authentic and happier.

This event wasn't so much about changing a belief, but rather deepening a belief. So clear and visceral was this lesson that there was no way I could ever go back on my principles again. From it, I received a whole different level of understanding that I now pass on to my own children.

To learn more about Vanna White, visit www.expertauthorpublishing.com/cob.

Right Under My Nose
Kay White

"So how tall is the shortest bloke you've been out with?" came the question from the front passenger seat. The cypress trees of the Italian countryside were flashing past as we sped down the motorway. I thought about it for a second and was happy I was wearing my dark sunglasses so the chap who asked the question couldn't see my eyes in his side mirror "Oh, about 5'10" I suppose."

The sun was wonderfully warm, the people with us in the car were warm too and the scenery was impossibly beautiful. It was easy to forget as I stared out of the window that I'd come along with "just a friend" of mine to make up the numbers for a long weekend break in Tuscany. I realized in that question, in that moment that perhaps—*in his mind anyway*—there could be more than friendship in the cards. Women have antennae for questions like that; well, I know I do.

Since I was 14, I've been 6 feet tall. As we grew up, all my friends stopped growing between about 5' 5" and 5' 8" and I just kept going. Whilst I've always been aware of being tall, I've also always enjoyed it. Mum made sure I stood up straight, and I never thought twice about wearing high heels if the occasion warranted it—or if I felt like it. I attracted taller boyfriends and, in truth, naturally scanned the scenery for taller men! They were obviously on my radar and, in short, as a tall woman, my boyfriends have always been as tall if not taller than I am. That's the way of things, isn't it?

Snowy (5' 5"), the chap in the front seat, had recently become a friend—as is often the case—through a mutual friend. Nick, who introduced us, was renting me a room in his house to tide me over. Snowy popped in to see Nick for a beer and a chat after being out on a somewhat dismal date. Snowy's real name is Simon. (With a surname of White, his nickname has always been Snowy or Chalky.) He and I compared bruised hearts and agreed how tricky it was to date; to find a date firstly and then, to find a date you actually *wanted* to date—and to juggle a career at the same time. I suggested that as two people licking their recent love wounds, we keep in touch to compare notes. "You tell me about your conquests and I'll give you the female spin, and you can give me the male spin on chaps I meet." A great arrangement I thought, and he emailed me a couple of days later suggesting lunch and a catch-up soon—all very nice, all very innocent and, as far as I was concerned, all very straightforward.

"We'll only be friends for heaven's sake," I said to my Mum when I told her I'd met a nice chap the other night. "He works in insurance, he's 5 years younger than me *and*—here's the end of it Mum—he's 7 inches shorter! Are those enough reasons "why not?" Mum agreed they were.

Snowy and I saw each other here and there for lunch, we made each other laugh, and whenever we met up I always felt really happy to see him. We chatted about anything and everything, and that included a chap I'd met at a party.

Snowy was very objective about him; he said it sounded as if he had a lot of baggage. "I mean, two kids and a second marriage behind him—what's that all about?" It was a good question, but I liked the bloke and having Snowy to bounce things around with was a bonus.

My friends were intrigued by the chap I was talking about more and more.

I'd noticed having fleeting feelings of disappointment here and there that Snowy and I could only ever be friends. Unless I could cut my legs off at the knees or spent my life sitting down—we just wouldn't be a fit, would we? I just couldn't see it or believe it could ever work. "I'm going to marry someone who's 6 feet or over, it's obvious isn't it?" I said to myself and to my friends who were intrigued by the chap I was talking about more and more. All the fairytales I'd ever read—or were read to me—had a handsome, taller-than-the-Princess Prince who saved the day and make her happy ever after. The end.

The truth was, Snowy decided fairly early on in our friendship that I was "the one." As far as he was concerned, rather than being 7 inches shorter, he was more than man enough for me. He knew he'd have the ultimate "look what I bagged" prize of a 6 foot blonde who made him laugh and made him feel like a giant!

Snowy and I have now been happily married for nearly 10 years. As Mrs. Kay White, I can honestly say I've never been happier, felt more loved and known what it truly means to have a life partner, soul mate and playmate all wrapped into one *cute* package. We have our fiery, feisty moments but then that's part of who we are and how we work together.

Snowy told me one night when we were "just friends" how he felt and how it was going to be, saying, "If ever you need anything, if ever I can do anything for you, I'll be there. You're the one for me and I'll make you so happy. I'll take anyone else on!" I'd said how special it was to hear that but it would *never* work. End of story.

A bit like in the canine world, the tall, leggy, long-nosed greyhounds tend to be placid but are able to run fast if ever needed. The terriers—and Jack Russells in particular—tend to be short, tenacious, plucky and full of character and fun. Well, this Greyhound married her Jack Russell, and if I hadn't changed that one belief that Mr. Right (or should I say Mr. White) had to be at least 6 feet tall, then I'd have missed the best thing that has ever happened to me. Truly I would, and that's the long and short of it.

I told the congregation on our wedding day that you don't always know when you've met *the one*. And on that strange day, there he was in Nick's kitchen; right under my nose—which is where, I hope, he'll always be.

Written Valentine's Day 2011
To learn more about Kay White, visit
www.expertauthorpublishing.com/cob.

Change The End of Your Story
Johnell Borer McCauley

When Pat picked up her husband John at the airport on that fateful Friday evening in 1980, she immediately knew something was wrong. John was returning from a long business trip and he looked tired, but this time it was different. John's face was drawn and ashen, he slouched when he walked, and he had no energy. He said that he just had a "touch of the flu" and would feel fine after some rest. Pat knew better.

First thing Monday morning, as they sat in the doctor's office, they learned it was even worse than either of them imagined. John had suffered a "silent" heart attack and needed immediate bypass surgery. Even with the surgery his chances of full recovery were very low. The doctor told him to "get his affairs in order." This, of course, is "doctor speak" for "we don't expect you to live much longer!"

Looking back, John's heart attack shouldn't have been a surprise. His great grandfather, his grandfather and his father all had heart attacks and died at an early age. End of story ... or was it?

Pat wasn't about to give up—this was her husband of 27 years and the man with whom she planned to spend the rest of her life.

Pat loved a challenge, and she loved John even more. When someone said nothing could be done, she tried even harder to find a solution and prove them wrong. In this case, she wasn't about to give up—this was her husband of 27 years and the man with whom she planned to spend the rest of her life. On top of that, he was the father of their nine children, with seven of them still under the age of 18 and living at home!

You see, John and Pat were my parents. I was married and pregnant with my first child (their first grandchild) when my dad had his heart attack. Instead of accepting the doctor's prognosis, they committed to changing the end of his story, and as a result, my story and the stories of my children and grandchildren. But, is it really possible to change the end of your story? You be the judge.

My dad took control of his health and lived another 16 active and healthy years. He got to know 19 of his grandchildren because of the changes he made. In turn, they had the gift of a grandfather in their lives. And, it all started by changing one belief. The whole family benefitted, not just from the extra years with him, but also from the things he and my mom shared with all of us as they became experts on the topic of good health.

One of the things that my parents learned was that only 20% of health issues come from our genetics. The other 80% are a result of lifestyle choices that we make. My parents also found many of the health issues that people think are genetic are actually a result of people practicing the same unhealthy habits they learned growing up. By changing the belief that his health was predetermined by genetics, my dad changed the end of his own story, and the stories of generations to come. How powerful is that?

When my dad came home after the surgery, everyone knew he was very sick but could also sense change was in the air. If Mom and Dad were switching things around, everyone was open to it. The food offered at the dining room table was very different, but the strategy for eating in a large family—finding something you like and grabbing it before it's gone—was the same!

Seven months after my dad's bypass surgery, I first held my new son in my arms. Like any new mother, I looked into my son's eyes and imagined his future. My parents had made the 400-mile trip to visit their very first grandchild in the hospital nursery. When I placed my son in my dad's arms for the first time, it became even clearer. There it was right in front of me—my past and my future. I made the decision right then and there to change my life. I didn't want something to happen to me because I didn't take care of myself—especially now that I knew how much difference taking action could make. I knew in that moment I would do everything I could to make sure that my family did not suffer with the health challenges of past generations.

I was already aware of how unhealthy habits could affect my own health. As a child, people politely told me that I was "big boned" and I "looked healthy." Of course, I now know that during my youth in the 1960s and 70s, these were "code words" for politely saying I was overweight. After the birth of my own child, I committed to following my dad's lead and changing the end of my story too.

I knew that fad diets and watching the scale did not work—I had tried that before. I needed a whole new approach to my health. I needed to change my habits. There were two key principles I took away from all that my parents learned—understand what you are eating, and make healthy choices each day. Once I learned these principles, I was able to pass them on to my children as healthy habits. They are now passing these same habits on to their children—or should I say my amazing grandchildren, who are the light of my life!

To learn more about Johnell Borer McCauley, visit www.expertauthorpublishing.com/cob.

Willo's Story
Gabriella Taylor

"Gabriella, Willo's calling and she sounds pretty upset." As I picked up the receiver to greet my best friend, I imagined she was weepy due to hormones, for she had given birth to her first baby three weeks earlier.

All I can hear are sobs on the line, "They're telling me I have four weeks to live." Something about a rare form of Leukemia, advanced stage, no known cure. At that point, I no longer hear words, I just feel sensations and it's hard to breathe.

When we first met, we remarked how our eyes were almost the same shade of green. I had been traveling the world and she became my first new friend once I returned to the United States. She was beautiful. Not a pert-nosed, pink-lipped beauty but more of an exotic bird with the sweetest smile in her clear eyes. Nearly six feet tall with an effortlessly taut, bronzed body, she was enchanting to watch. We fell in love with one another instantly.

Fast-forward ahead three years from that fateful phone call. Through radiation treatments, chemotherapy and an excruciating bone marrow transplant, we were told she would perhaps live to see her little girl grow.

On Valentine's Day, I received another call saying that a grapefruit sized mass was found and she was being hospitalized indefinitely. By this point, I had moved to

San Francisco. I made immediate plans to move back to Oregon temporarily to be with her.

I was 28 years old sitting at the hospital bedside of my 32-year old friend, watching her body deteriorate. She alternated between being so swollen from steroids it looked as if her skin would burst were she pricked by a pin, and revealing her emaciated frame, seeming as fragile as a rice paper lamp. A shocking hole was carved in her face the size of a fist to remove her right eye due to a virus she acquired in ICU. As her body shut down, she hovered in a coma-like sleep punctuated by moments of startling lucidity.

I spent hours reflecting upon my life as her body disintegrated before my eyes. I had suffered a long withstanding love/hate relationship with my body. I began dieting at the tender age of eight. By 14 years old, I was hospitalized repeatedly for eating disorder related behavior. I had attempted suicide twice as my despair was so great. I'd slave my way to be thin, then I'd binge on Peanut Butter and Fluff sandwiches in misery.

I wanted to feel at home in my own skin, I just didn't know how to get there

I gave up believing that peace with my body was possible and resigned myself to enduring this silent hell as my personal cross to bear. I wanted to feel at home in my own skin, I just didn't know how to get there nor did anyone else seem able to show me, despite thousands of dollars and hours spent in therapy.

That May, Willo miraculously regained her strength and stabilized. She was permitted to go home for the first time in four months.

During that time, we would bring her daughter Sequoia to pick the wild concord grapes that grew in her front yard. We would get excited about the Morel mushrooms at the farmers market and prepare delicious meals—I had my friend back. I sensed it was temporary, yet I felt I was given permission to stop waiting for her to die.

One night, we were chatting on her bed and she was asking me what was going on with me. I had been engaged in yet another inner battle to lose weight, as all of this time in the hospital was stressful and I sought comfort in the salty sweet forms of tortilla chips and chocolate. I was lamenting how I had noticed my pants were getting tight and I felt fat, despite the morning spin classes I would take at the gym next to the hospital.

She sat upright and looked at me, no she looked *into* me, with that one piercing green eye of hers and said, "Gabriella, you can't play that game anymore. I am going to die soon, I'm going to leave my baby girl without a mom, and my body will be gone. You just don't have time for this fight anymore. Promise me that you will use my death as a catalyst for you to live like you've never lived before."

I knew in my heart how true her words were as the surging impulse to rise up inside of myself became stronger than any petty tug to play small. In that moment, the belief that my body was a burden was transmuted into an awareness that it was a miraculous gift that permitted me life. It was my choice to cooperate with this or not.

I became my own research project—how does one actually make peace with beauty, coming out from years of body blame into the dawn of genuine self-acceptance?

Thus, my greatest love and area of expertise were revealed to me. I later created the precise roadmap that worked to free myself of this quiet tyranny. Not only do I now reside largely in a place of sweet peace with my body, I know how to pick myself up when I stumble. I now teach these principles because I believe so strongly in their importance.

Willo died three weeks later in her mom's arms. Before the coroner came for her body, her daughter and I gathered roses from outside her window. We rubbed our tears and rose oil into her skin, sprinkling the petals over her lifeless form as an homage to the unspeakably beautiful light that shone within her.

To learn more about Gabriella Taylor, visit www.expertauthorpublishing.com/cob.

Fishing Feels Better
Carter Peel

A couple of years ago, when I was 11, I really wanted to go see "Ironman" with my brother, Logan, so I asked my dad for $50. When Dad asked why I wanted the money, I told him I wanted to take Logan to Burger King and a movie. Rather than just giving me the money, he asked me what I thought I could do to earn it. I said I didn't know. My stepmom, Tammi, said to keep my eyes and ears open for things I could do to help around the house, so I did. The next night when Dad and Tammi were making dinner I asked if I could help. That weekend when Dad started cleaning the garage, I asked if I could help. When I would see one of them starting to unload the dishwasher I would tell them to sit down and I would do it for them. Once I even asked if I could rub my Dad's feet after a long day at work. Dad started giving me an allowance and I thought that was really cool.

One day when my stepmom was getting ready to have a party at her gallery, I asked if I could come too. She said sure. It was a fun night at the gallery and people were talking, laughing and having a good time. As I was standing around, I heard this lady say she was thirsty, so I asked her if I could get her a soda or some water, she laughed and said I was cute. Then she said yes, she would love a soda. So I went and got it and when I handed it to her, she tried to give me a dollar, I said "No, that's okay." Then the man she was talking to said he would like some hot tea, so I got him a cup of tea. He offered me some money too, but I said "No thank you." I did not want my stepmom or my Dad to get mad at me.

Later Tammi asked if I was having fun, I said yes. I told her I had gotten a couple of people drinks and they tried to give me money, but I couldn't take it because I didn't want her or Dad mad at me. Tammi told me it would be fine to graciously receive what was being offered, but not to ask or expect anything from anyone. I was kind of excited! So I started going around to the people at the party and asking if they wanted something to drink and I started helping them. Some people gave me quarters, some gave me dollars and some people did not give me anything, but it didn't matter, I was just having fun and helping. I also really liked it when I made people laugh. By the end of the night my feet hurt, but I was happy. And I was really, REALLY happy when I got home and counted all the money that everyone had given me. I made 37 dollars all on my own!

I spent more time thinking about what I really wanted.

Later that week, my Dad and I were at the store and I asked him if he would buy me a video game. Dad reminded me about the money I had earned and said if I really wanted it I could buy it for myself. I thought about it and decided I didn't really want it that bad. Somehow it was different spending my own money instead of my Dad's. I found I was more picky and cautious about spending my own money. I also spent more time thinking about what I really wanted.

The next week I asked my stepmom if I could come back to her gallery and work some more and she said sure. One day we got home after working for a long time, I told her my feet felt broken, but it was worth it, because I liked the feeling of making my own money. She laughed and gave me another $10.

I used to think I wanted people to do things for me, give me money and buy me things... but I have changed my mind about that. I now know it feels much better to work hard, do things on my own, help others, and make my own money than it does to just be handed things. My Dad told me something about being given a fishing pole rather than just a fish. He also said he is so proud of me, my work ethic, and that I learned these lessons early in life. And you know what? I am too!

To learn more about Carter Peel, visit www.expertauthorpublishing.com/cob.

A Root Lesson
Rex Bohachewski

It was the middle of summer, and a day that would influence my whole life, but it started as just another sunny morning with blue sky and a warm breeze. I was 12 years old and more interested in appreciating the warm weather than I was in helping my dad clear land at the back of our property. We lived on a farm and were clearing a wooded area for more cow pasture.

Dad was on the bulldozer and leveling the ground where we had recently removed several trees. It was my job to pick up any roots that were uncovered as he moved the dirt. As dad was on the bulldozer, he was able to cover more ground faster than I could, especially since I didn't want to be there in the first place. He was uncovering tree roots more quickly than I could pick them up. My motivation and desire to do a good job were extremely low. I started to express these thoughts to my dad, but all he did was point out from his seat the roots I had missed as he kept leveling.

I was aware I had a choice—and I chose to enjoy the work I was doing.

I suddenly realized, standing in the middle of that field with a root in my hand, that I would be working for the rest of my life. Being 12, I calculated that I would probably be working until 50, meaning that I had 38 more years of work ahead of me. Now, it followed that those years of work would be over three times as long as I had lived so far! I understood I could either not like work and have a long and miserable life, or I could take satisfaction in whatever job I was doing, and have a happier life. I was aware I had a choice—and I chose to enjoy the work I was doing.

Immediately I looked for a way to make the task at hand more pleasurable, and the first thing I thought of was making it easier. So instead of running around like a chicken with its head cut off, I analyzed how to cover the same area with less effort. The result was placing a mental grid over the area, covering it systematically, and going over the ground only once. Fewer steps made it easier for me, therefore I enjoyed it more, and I did a better job getting all the roots, making Dad happier.

Homework, my chores, and any work thereafter received the same mental attitude adjustment. It didn't matter whether I was cutting the lawns, putting up a fence with dad during Spring Break, feeding the cows, bringing in the wood, cleaning the barns, weeding the garden, picking corn at the neighbor's place, or washing dishes as a part-time job, that new mental view served me extremely well. I did all jobs to the best of my ability and with a positive attitude, looking at them as learning experiences that would lead me to greater things.

Later when I was at university I saw a document posted on a board at the side of a classroom. I read it and then copied it down. I include it here as it confirmed what I had first learned that fateful summer day. The following was written by Charles Swindoll, who is a Church minister in Abbotsford, B.C. and is entitled "Attitude":

The longer I live, the more I realize the impact of attitude on life.

Attitude, to me, is more important than facts. It is more important than the past, than education, than money, than circumstances, than failures, than successes, than what other people think or say or do. It is more important than appearance, giftedness or skill. It will make or break a company...a church...a home.

The remarkable thing is we have a choice every day regarding the attitude we will embrace...We cannot change our past...we cannot change the fact that people will act in a certain way. We cannot change the inevitable. The only thing we can do is play on the one string we have, and that is our attitude...I am convinced that life is 10% what happens to me and 90% how I react to it.

And so it is with you...we are in charge of our attitudes.

These words sum up the positive outlook I adopted so many years ago—and I am thankful my attitude has benefitted not only my career, but <u>all</u> areas of my life.

To learn more about Rex Bohachewski, visit www.expertauthorpublishing.com/cob.

Gypsy Mermaid of the Rockies
Marina Mermaid

It all started with a toothbrush. In 1995 I fell madly in love with an electrician who worked in Banff. I met him in Quebec while visiting a friend. Back in Montreal, he drove all the way from Quebec in a snowstorm to bring me the toothbrush I left behind. He walked in with the toothbrush in his mouth at a rakish angle and a twinkle in his eye. How could I resist?

I sold my furniture and humble belongings and off I went. I followed this magnetic Bad Boy Dude with dreadlocks who was living in his flower power '68 Chevy with his white husky "Chinook." My mom was terrified. She thought I would die crossing Canada in that old piece of metal. I had no money and I did not speak English very well, but I was a Gypsy Mermaid looking for an ocean of change and a wave of prosperity.

In Wawa, Ontario we lost our front wheel and the engine died. I paid for repairs with my credit card. His van was finished in plywood with no comforts inside. We washed ourselves in campgrounds, cooked in parks, and I cleaned the dishes in public washrooms.

In Banff I got a husky puppy of my own I named Vedder because I was grunge-crazy for Pearl Jam's Eddie Vedder. My dude was a pothead and his friends were French Canadian ski bums. But one of my big goals was to learn English. Oh well, I had freedom to the max! Nobody knew me in Banff. I had no phone, no pager, no address. The police hassled us regularly because we parked illegally, slept anywhere we wanted, and our dogs had no licenses. For once in my life I was a Gypsy with no responsibilities.

One night one of the dogs became severely sick from his pet food and could not hold it anymore. At 3 a.m. he sprayed us royally with diarrhea. We were drenched and covered from head to toe. We hosed ourselves and the inside of the van with cold water. Bad Boy drove me to the laundromat and then went to work. I washed all of our belongings, feeling ashamed. Time to clean up, Gypsy Mermaid.

We finally moved into a modified shed in someone's backyard. Unpacking, I noticed his prized possessions were his pet and the pot plant he placed in the kitchen window.

Days later, I found cocaine under the floorboards. I knew he was hiding it for his best friend, Jim, freshly out of jail on probation. Jim's family cut a deal for him, giving him a chance to rebuild his life in Banff. They even moved there to support him. His father was an ex-police officer. My own sister was a narc in Montreal. I decided I loved myself too much to take any risks. I told Jim's dad, "Your son is still trafficking drugs, and making us accomplices."

That night I confronted my boyfriend with what I had done and I saw the coldness in his eyes. Gypsy Mermaid was not loved. He was more concerned about Jim, and I was afraid Jim would beat me up.

That night I couldn't sleep. At 5:00 a.m., my boyfriend went to work and I packed up my stuff and headed to my friend Wanda's. At her place, I'd lie under the stairs on a mattress in a fetal position thinking, *I'm safe now. I'm safe.* But I still wanted to flee. I was too scared to notice things were already turning around. Wanda was my only English-speaking friend and the sole person to take me in. I was getting what I wanted—to learn English.

My boyfriend never came to look for me, even just to see if I was okay. I felt like a nobody, and here I was in love with him!

Wanda took me to a clinic where the psychologist asked me, "Marina, are you going to leave Banff because you're afraid of this guy? You have a right to be here." I had a job and was saving money so I could learn Shiatsu massage in Japan, then move to Vancouver. "This is your dream we're talking about," she added, "Are you going to let this guy ruin your dream by escaping and hiding?" She gave me some Valium so I could sleep.

The next day I woke up and knew I would not be taking Valium. I had to find another way. So I biked every day through the Rockies, to the Hoodoos, yellow cliffs overlooking the Bow River. I would go there and just breathe, watching eagles swoop and glide.

I began to appreciate Banff, knowing how lucky I was to be there. I forced myself to connect and be in nature. I was always afraid of being alone in the woods or by myself on a trail. I would never go camping alone, I had to feel safe and protected. These rides helped me to connect with what I needed to be safe and happy.

I did not need the protection of a man, I could be on my own and be safe.

I would stand on the cliff and open my arms, looking up at the sky. It became my ritual. I was hesitant at first: *Is there anybody looking?* In those moments of quiet connectedness, I received more strength than I expected. I did not need the protection of a man, I could be on my own and be safe.

I made the decision to stick around, and in six months I did everything I wanted—I saved the money and left for Japan. I was forced to dive into the culture and learn Japanese and English at the same time, since nobody spoke French. The best way to learn is to teach, so I got a job teaching children English three days a week. Adults would laugh at me for my accent and choice of words, but those kids did not judge. In the afternoons I went to Shiatsu school for two years.

After moving to Vancouver, I found a place to live, got an agent, started to work on movie sets as a stand-in, and promoted my massage to the film industry. With my massage practice, I found freedom again—within a structure.

I ran into Jim, his father and his girlfriend on the street one day. I was so surprised that they were nice to me. His girlfriend was now his wife. I thought, *maybe I did him a favor.* I changed his life, and he changed mine. He had given me a gift—the gift of myself.

To learn more about Marina Mermaid, visit www.expertauthorpublishing.com/cob.

Growing Up by Slimming Down
Lorenzo Lamas

My earliest memories are of the Pacific Palisades area where I grew up in Los Angeles. My mother purchased a house near Will Rogers State Park after she divorced my dad and remarried. It was completely like Mayberry RFD, a very normal neighborhood where I could go down the street and hang out with my best friends at seven or eight years old. In the summertime I would stay out until 9:00 or 10:00 playing stickball, frisbee and riding bikes. On weekends we would grab canteens, sandwiches and fruit and go hiking for hours in the Santa Monica Mountains. It was very safe—a completely different world in the late 60s.

Two or three times a week my father would pick me up from public school and head for the Bel Air house he shared with his wife Esther Williams. Of course it had a big pool and everybody would swim. That was a very sheltered and wonderful life where I had access to both parents. I feel so fortunate to have so many memories growing up in the safety net of those two neighborhoods.

Then my mom divorced her husband and was hired by a New York cosmetics company. She was advised that Manhattan would be a better place to learn the business. So one summer day in 1971 when I was 13 years old, my mom told me we were moving to New York. I would be going to a summer camp and then Admiral Farragut Academy, a naval military school.

I stuffed my feelings and I started eating.

The school was in Pine Beach, New Jersey, a billion miles away from California, all my friends and my dad. I had no choice; I had to go along with it. I thought it might be better if I did have to go away to boarding school and not live with my mom if I couldn't see my dad. Maybe that would be like living on my own. I didn't want to live with my mom in New York because that would hurt my dad, and if I moved in with my dad, that would hurt my mom. I stuffed my feelings, and the anxiety of the separation made me increasingly depressed. I started eating.

At 13 I gained 35 or 40 pounds in about a year. At the end of my freshman year of high school I was 5'4" and 160 pounds with a 38-inch waist. I didn't like military school but I felt like I had to stick it out, so I kept eating. By the end of my sophomore year, I was 5'5" and 185 pounds. I was never picked to participate in squad teams for baseball, football or any other sport. I was terrible at physical activities because I was so fat I couldn't run. Kids would make fun of me and I would get pushed around. It was an awful time that took me deeper and deeper into self-pity.

It's hard when you're so young to be away from home. But when you're with a bunch of guys in the same predicament, you tend to bond with them and they become your family. We were basically a bunch of orphans wearing uniforms, marching around and trying to get good grades so we could go into town on the weekend and see a movie. I became very resilient and I adjusted—I was also lucky to have a best friend named Kendall.

One day I was looking in the mirror while changing and I got so disgusted, so grossed out looking at myself, that I decided to stop wishing I had a physique like my best friend or that I could run as fast as the track star in my class and do something about it. I remembered back in the Palisades my mother would wake up early sometimes and do exercises with Jack LaLanne on TV. I'd do them with her a couple of days a week for 20 minutes before school. My mom was always physically active. She had to remain limber because she did stage shows. I missed exercising with her so I sent away for Jack LaLanne's 5-Minute Body Shaper, which had cables and pulleys you'd attach to a doorknob to do scissor kicks, side bends and sit-ups. I'd use it for 20 minutes after evening mess and before study hall. My friends would make fun of me but I didn't care. I also borrowed a book from my mom on one of two weekends a month I went home. I read *The Atkins Diet* cover to cover. I was so happy to find I could easily eat my favorite foods and still lose weight.

So here I am, 15 years old and motivated. I'm going to change the way I look. I'm eating better, I'm using that Body Shaper and within four months, I'm beginning to look better.

My waist goes from 38 to 34. Some of my friends begin to notice I'm more physically fit. I can do a push-up, which I couldn't do before. By the end of six months I do a couple of pull-ups, previously impossible. I'd failed the

Marine Corps physical fitness test at my school every time, and now I was able to pass because I decided I wasn't going to feel sorry for myself anymore. I was taking steps to better my life and the way I felt about myself.

When I got a little bit more confidence, I went out for wrestling and made the team. This meant I was forced to work out for two hours a day after school for about three months. In my junior year I made JV, and I made Varsity my senior year. Then I went out for track. I had never been able to run more than 50 yards without stopping to catch my breath. In my senior year I ran in the 880-yard dash, nailed the high jump and threw the discus.

My life was changed forever that one winter day at military school looking in the mirror and deciding I was sick of being fat. I was tired of wishing I were somebody else. I knew if I made the effort I could change myself.

Everybody can do it. There's not one person on the planet who can't do what I did. It's not magic. It's just a commitment to think differently about food and exercise.

All through school, Kendall was my best friend. He was a great athlete; he was on the football team, track team and wrestling team. He knew me better than anybody and he was proud of what I did.

Just before we started our senior year, I returned early with the other student officers for officer's training, drilling and learning commands to give the cadets. Kendall was also an officer and we had written each other and made plans to catch up. As I'm walking across the concrete courtyard on the first day, I see Kendall heading toward me. We hadn't seen each other since June. Over the summer I worked at McDonald's in Santa Monica, riding my bike to work from my dad's in Beverly Hills, then to the beach for a swim, then back home—about three miles every day.

By the time I got to officer training, I looked like an athlete—I was 6 feet tall, in great shape and about 170 pounds. As I was about to pass Kendall, I almost stuck out my hand to wave but I didn't. We walked right by each other and he didn't even recognize me! I turned around and said, "Yo, Kendall, what's up?"

He looked at me, shocked, and said, "Lorenzo?"

"Yeah, who do you think it is?"

"What happened?"

That was the moment I felt the most proud. I knew from then on that my life would be different; that I would feel more confident around girls, that in my senior year I would kick ass in track and it would be awesome. And it was.

I was self-assured in social situations, I started coming out of my shell, I even did better in school because I started to ask questions and participate. I didn't mind the attention anymore. When I was fat I couldn't stand being the center of attention, I just wanted to crawl under a rock. Now I felt much less isolated, like I was part of the world.

Once you start working out and seeing a change in your body it's a bit addicting. You want to keep working and changing even more. I came back to California after I graduated, stayed with Dad and Esther and got a job at a Jack LaLanne health spa. I went from being this dumpy kid to coaching people and helping them change their own images and confidence levels.

    I credit that school with making me tough when things weren't going well in life, causing me to dig deep to figure it out. Even though adjusting to military school at that young age was the hardest thing I have ever done in my whole life, the adversity I overcame gave me the foundation to meet the challenges that life has thrown at me.

To learn more about Lorenzo Lamas, visit www.expertauthorpublishing.com/cob.

Our South African Awakening
Brian Leslie

On the flight down to South Africa we huddled together with worries slowly building. My wife nudged me, "Brian, are you sure we can do this? What if something ... happens?" I had my own misgivings too but needed to stay positive. "We will be just fine, Sweetie. I hear we have a lovely company house in a nice area and Sabie is very safe." I tried to keep the doubt out of my voice. Was this the right thing to do? What was I dragging us into?

The headhunter had assured me that this was a great project. "It couldn't be safer!" he had said. However, the South Africans I spoke to later had told me otherwise. "Crime is rampant, especially in the townships. Don't trust those blacks!"

It was the spring of 2001, only seven years after the end of apartheid. Nelson Mandela was president. Desmond Tutu was in the middle of his truth and reconciliation commission. The blacks had taken power with a democratically elected government and a very peaceful transition seemed to be occurring. Dr. Tutu's commission had exposed the sins of apartheid and the true horror of what the repression had created. However, despite this, forgiveness was the order of the day. There was no bloodbath. There was no revolution. There was no social unrest. However, we had been told (by white ex-South Africans) to expect otherwise.

We arrived in Sabie to a gated, alarmed, motion scanned and double locked home. Our neighbors were vociferous in their warnings, "Stay away from them bleks. Stay out of Simile Township." We didn't need to be reminded. We were convinced that despite truth and reconciliation, the blacks were dangerous. There was all that simmering anger left from apartheid.

I was working on a United Nations Development Program project helping establish local management in a forest company. Anne wanted to volunteer. She was a teacher and there was a critical need for teachers in the area. What a shame she couldn't go to the township, where the most needy schools were! Anne settled on doing any type of volunteer work, as long as it was safe.

I arranged for Anne and I to meet Sister Gloria a couple of weeks after we arrived. I had been told she was a good person to suggest safe volunteer work. She was the company nursing sister and the caregiver for 800 plus men, many who were dealing with HIV/AIDS. She was a force to reckon with and she had a long list of what she termed "safe and useful" volunteer jobs. "What do you do, Anne?" asked Sister Gloria. "Teach," said Anne. "Well, do I have a useful job for you! Come with me!" she replied. With that they were off, climbing into a rusty old Toyota and heading directly toward Simile. I stood there envisioning Anne. She must be feeling so alarmed. She had never met the woman before. Was she being hijacked? What was going to happen?

That evening when I arrived home for dinner, there sat Anne with a huge grin on her face. "I got a job today," she announced coyly. "You what? What happened? I thought you were being kidnapped!" She then began to explain. "When we arrived at Acme School in the township, we met an energetic and friendly man named John Sambo—the school principal. I must admit that I was looking around nervously ... but suddenly Mr. Sambo was welcoming me to his school. He is a *very* cheerful man and, I might add, certainly no one who would make you uncomfortable. I told him about my teaching experience and he immediately took me to a classroom filled with children. He explained that they had not had a teacher for three months. Well, when I saw the children, my fears evaporated! The classroom was bright and airy and the children amazing. Sweetie, I love it! I agreed to stay for the remaining three months of the term!"

I let that sink in. My wife would be working in the township for three months? "How will you get there?" I asked. "The Toyota Camry," said Anne. She quickly added, "Mr. Sambo said it would be fine." Dubious, I answered, "Are you sure it's safe?" Anne replied with enthusiasm, "Yes, yes, Simile looks fine, and Sister Gloria assured me that there would be no problem."

Communication was a challenge, but they were overjoyed to have a teacher.

So despite my misgivings, my dear wife took on 43 children in a class up in the local township. They spoke mainly Sesotho, Tsonga, or Siswati. Communication was a challenge, but they were overjoyed to have a teacher—and a white woman no less! This had never happened.

Anne found them wonderful. They were eager to learn and attentive. She was amazed when a deluge of rain arrived and the children rose en masse, scurrying to find pots and containers to catch the drips. At the end of each day, without any comment, they grabbed pails and rags and washed their class top to bottom. When school was over, Anne was touched to go out and find that her car had been washed and shined. Against many protests from our neighbors she had driven her Toyota Camry into Simile. "You'll be sorry," they had warned. However, Anne discovered completely the opposite. Her car was more secure in Simile than anywhere else in the town. The children and their parents appreciated her help so much that they took extra care to make her feel welcome and safe.

Anne spent six months working at the Acme School and enjoyed every single day. Her heart warmed when she wandered through town and a little waif of a child called out, "Hi, Missus Leslie!" or when she arrived at school to find a polished shiny stone left on her desk as a token of appreciation and respect. Her experience was truly rich and made more so by the fact that it was not what either of us had believed would happen. Not in our wildest dreams!

To learn more about Brian Leslie, visit www.expertauthorpublishing.com/cob.

Driving Towards Joy
Nancy Peet

It has always been a dream of mine to travel aimlessly in New Zealand. For years I yearned to be in the lush, damp greenness of her mossy hills. I imagined what it would be like to listen to the birds and swim with the seals. I finally manifested a way to make it happen. My plan was to spend a year living in a campervan. That way, I could do as I pleased and go where the wind took me. It would be my ultimate adventure.

I flew into Christchurch, and planned on staying just long enough to find my perfect home on wheels. Each day, I got a newspaper, then walked and bused all over the city. I looked at potential homes and went on test drives. Day after day, I pounded the pavement. Nothing felt right. The days became weeks. I was getting frustrated, and I was slowly losing my sense of adventure. All I wanted was to be on a beach somewhere and be free. This had been my fantasy for so long, yet here I was, getting more miserable with each moment.

I longed to be out on the Earth so badly that I ached. The city was the last place I wanted to be. Here I was in this gorgeous country, yet I was disconnected from the land I wanted to embrace. How could I leave the city without my van? I had three suitcases packed full of stuff. I couldn't carry it all, or even take it on a bus comfortably, so on I plodded. Looking at wrong van after wrong van.

One day I went to a notice board to see if there was anything new, and a sign caught my eye. A drive-away company was looking for someone to bring a car to a small town on the sea, five hours north. I instantly felt a flutter of excitement at the possibility of getting out of there. But that was stupid! If I couldn't find wheels in a city, how would I ever find them in a small town? It seemed so completely illogical. The smell of surf and freedom that had just wisped its alluring tendrils past my nose was gone in an instant.

Every time I would think of that town, I would feel that same flutter of happiness. Yet each time, I would tell myself it was the wrong thing to do.

The next day, I went back to the board. There was the same sign. Beckoning me. Again, I felt the excitement and then I shut it out. I turned away and felt my body slump in resignation. I sat under a tree to have a good cry. The voice of authority was having it out with the voice of possibility. I was able to stand back and witness this battle within me for the first time. I thought, "What is this voice of authority? And why do I give it so much obedience? Why is logic always better?" It didn't seem to be getting me anywhere. I had been here for three weeks, and the only thing I had to show for it was frustration and detachment.

I looked at this belief, head on. I saw myself as a free spirit, but under certain circumstances I played it safe, even when playing it safe wasn't working. Did I trust my intuition? —Apparently not. I had been blindly following all the advice I had read on how to buy a vehicle in New Zealand, and my joy was dwindling more each day. Couldn't I change my mind, right then and there? Wouldn't following my joy at least break up this monotony? I decided that even if I didn't find a van in that small town on the sea, I'd figure something out. I had to follow my joy!

> *I giggled and sang and bounced around*
> *on the "wrong" side of the road.*

Off I drove in my shiny new car, heading north. I couldn't imagine how this decision would bring me my home on wheels, but I was free! That was all that mattered. The rest would work itself out. I giggled and sang and bounced around on the "wrong" side of the road. I walked barefoot down many beaches that I knew I'd come back to later. I had two days of exploring my new life.

After I dropped the car off, I moved into a small, beautiful hostel. I found the local paper, and there was an ad for a van that sounded perfect. One hour after arriving, I had already made an appointment for the next day.

The van was perfect! It had been custom built by a retired couple, and they had spared no expense. They were selling it cheap just because they were kind. The van had everything I could have dreamed of, and more.

When I went to bring them the money and drive away, they invited me in for dinner. They were such lovely people. They asked what I needed to buy. Everything! Into the cupboards and closets they went.

Blankets, towels, pillows, pots and pans, dishes, silverware, salt and pepper shakers, a clothesline and clothespins, filled water jugs. Then there was the food: veggies from their garden, fruit from their trees, olive oil, homemade jam, local honey, a cooler to put it all in. They even gave me an old cd player, a fan, and a folding chaise lounge for the beach.

They also gave me a sense of family. We stayed in touch, and I went back to visit them many times. I parked in their driveway for a rest from the road. They cooked for me and insisted on doing my laundry. I fell in love with them.

I have learned to recognize when I am doing something that is slowly draining me of joy. This often happens because I am doing something I feel I should do. I sniff the air for a scent of the New Zealand sea, in order to find which way my joy is. When I find it, I drive towards it. With the windows rolled down. Singing loudly.

To learn more about Nancy Peet, visit
www.expertauthorpublishing.com/cob.

Loving is a Choice
Rebecca Skeele

There was no place to run or hide. I had to stand there and take it. "You have ruined your children's lives and they will never forgive you. How could you break up the family?"

These harsh words brought stinging tears to my eyes. The blood rushed out of my body and my knees felt weak. I stood frozen at the kitchen sink where I had been doing dishes, paralyzed by the intensity of the condemnation. In this moment I recognized the blaming and shaming voice was none other than my own! I felt myself leaning on the counter for support. Where had I learned to be so cruel?

It all started with my decision to end my 10-year marriage. For months I had tried to deny the small but persistent voice in my heart that whispered, "It's over." I dreaded the disapproval, judgment and rejection I assumed would come my way from well-meaning but ill-informed family and friends. However, I found I was my hardest critic during that difficult time. I told myself I was the one who had broken the unspoken family code that dictated I stay in the marriage no matter what.

My then-husband and I had been doing a convincing job playing house, shielding our kids from the breakdown of our marital relationship. They were four and seven at the time and completely taken by surprise when we told them about the divorce. We decided to keep their routines as regular as possible for the months left until summer break. We each took a turn spending a week at the house. Striving for normalcy, we kept them in the same bedrooms, the same school, and with the friends they knew. Like many kids, they were devastated by the divorce. The most difficult thing for me was being away from the house when I was used to being a mom all the time. I believed I deserved to feel miserable.

I heard that terrible voice out loud one day when I said to a friend, "I know it was all my fault. How could I have been so selfish?" There it was, the "S" word. How often had my mother accused me of being selfish as a young girl when I was trying to assert my own voice, or name my own choices, or decide from my heart? In fact, as an adult, I was still defensive and reactive around my mother. I thought, "Wait a minute. Was I really being selfish when I decided to end my marriage?" Again I heard that soft voice in my heart: "No. I want to experience the truth about love." What could that possibly mean? Love was about the other: finding love, seeking love, waiting for love. Wasn't that the truth? How was I going to find out the truth about love?

The year of the divorce, when summer break came, the kids and I were able to explore my new place together. We got to know the neighborhood. They adjusted and even began to make some new friends there. The effort to keep them on an even keel had been worth it.

Later, I went through an intensive healing program. I still sought love's true nature. The course focused on self-acceptance and self-forgiveness. The facilitators suggested I was my toughest judge, and the cause of much of the intense unhappiness I was feeling. The moment when I had been washing dishes and recognized that harsh voice as my own came rushing back. I realized that inner voice was still very loud. It described me with terms like selfish, vengeful, awful, self-condemning, miserable, socially outcast, emotionally exiled, and inexcusable. I also felt stuck as my rational mind questioned the ideas of self-acceptance and self-forgiveness at every turn. I had to get out of my head. I needed to listen to my heart. I came to realize my heart's voice might not have the volume of that cruel voice, but it had a quality to it that was unmistakably compassionate and loving. This was the beginning of breaking down the beliefs that had held me hostage for so long.

Gradually, I began to learn how to focus on my inner voice of compassion instead of the hurtful voice. I worked through the healing program and began to meditate and journal regularly. I realized like a bird in a tree, a feeling just is. My heart warmed up to that truth. I began to find it easier to tune into the accepting, forgiving, loving voice of my true self.

Eventually, I was able to open my heart.

I remember a big moment for me when I was talking to my mother on the phone. She was doing her best to support me, yet she was disapproving. She was questioning me about how things were going and how the kids were doing. I recall her voice had a certain tone to it, somewhere between "I'm really concerned about you" and "I'm judging you and don't approve of what you're doing <u>and</u> I'm really concerned about you." I remember being able to observe, accept, and forgive myself for whatever was coming up in that moment. I did not get defensive. I did not get reactive. I could hear the concern in her voice. I said, "Mom, I know you're really concerned about the kids and about me and everything and I need you to know I'm okay. I'm really okay." After that call, I took a nice deep breath, exhaled, and thought, "Whoa, glad that's over!" It was great. I felt I had maintained my sense of my own truth. I was not focusing on inner blame or shame just because I had heard disapproval in my mother's voice. I had come a long way since feeling paralyzed while doing dishes at the kitchen sink.

Eventually, I was able to open my heart, accept the feelings and forgive the self-judgments. I realized my inner wellbeing was my choice and my happiness didn't depend on receiving love from others.

The truth about love? Love comes from inside me. Love is who I am.

To learn more about Rebecca Skeele, visit www.expertauthorpublishing.com/cob.

When One Door Closes, Another One Opens
Holly Eburne

As a certified Sport Physiotherapist and health and wellness coach for 30 years, I had the good fortune to travel all over the world with Canadian National athletes, including the National Waterskiing Team. Over the years, I have worked with professional hockey, soccer and football organizations.

I was inspired by the athletes' work ethic and commitment to do the best they could every time, whether in a practice or an actual game.

I am, by nature, an achiever too, and one of my major life goals was to work with Olympic athletes at the Olympic games. I was on track to achieving this goal and in June 2006 I was asked to be an assistant Physiotherapist for the Canadian Freestyle Ski Team for the 2010 Olympics. Then my life took a sudden detour—my husband Dave was diagnosed with Frontotemporal Dementia in March of 2007. He was only 57.

The dreams we had for our lives together were shattered. At first I couldn't believe it, and then I quickly put on my "tough" exterior, determined to travel the road of dementia with ease.

Two years later, after filling every second with "busyness," I hit a wall. I was exhausted and I honestly didn't know how I was going to survive the situation. Dave was doing quite well from the care I was giving him, but I was slipping. I was sad and resentful of the curve ball that life threw at me during the peak years of my life.

Hadn't I gone through enough challenges with the passing of my mom, my sister, and a daughter with serious health issues? On top of this, I learned that all of our savings (35 years' worth) had collapsed.

I've never asked, "Why did this happen to me?" But I have felt resentment. This isn't what I expected my life to be—this is not how I envisioned our future together. And I was also dealing with the loneliness and pain of losing emotional and physical intimacy with my husband.

Less than a month later, I had a turning point. I was standing in the kitchen cooking dinner and hating it. Dave was always the cook. I did cleanup duty. I wanted to slam the knife into the cutting board, walk out of the house and let someone else take over. I crumpled over the counter, stifling my tears so Dave wouldn't hear them. Then, all of a sudden, a thought hit me from out of the blue.

I realized I had a choice: I could stay in my angry, "poor me" state, or move forward. In that moment, I felt I was sitting in the last row of Life's Touring Bus—next to the bathroom. I was fed up with the odor and I needed and wanted to find a way back into the driver's seat.

I knew I had to make radical changes because my old ways were no longer working.

I was also letting myself *feel* for the first time since the diagnosis—I had awareness of how miserable I truly was. I'm usually a joyful person, and I desperately wanted to find my way back to myself. I didn't know *how*

I was going to do it, but I knew I had to make radical changes because my old ways were no longer working for me.

That night I started a gratitude journal.

The next morning I went for a run, and I made sure that every single day I did some form of exercise. I had been exercising three to four times a week, now it was every day.

Once I committed to it, I made certain I took action, not only with fitness, but eating better and hydrating. I began to clear space in my house, making filing systems and becoming more organized so I could make life run smoothly—easy and inspired solutions I could later share with clients. *And I made the ultimate choice: to put myself first. If I did not do this, I was not going to survive—and I would take my husband and my two children down with me.*

In 2008, I phoned the head therapist for the National Freestyle Ski team and said I wasn't sure if I would be able to work for the full time required—five weeks.

In June 2009, I made my final decision to pull my Olympic application—and I did it with full awareness of what it meant. I had let go of a goal that I thought was the most powerful goal I could set—other than having children.

But by now, I had a new perspective. I had to ask myself some questions. How would Dave manage if I were away for five weeks? Would I be okay with staying home and watching the Olympics on TV? I discovered there wasn't any question—the answer became obvious. There was no way that I could be away for that long.

I had spent over half of my life on this goal—traveling with national teams, volunteering thousands of hours—but would I be remembered for going to the Olympics when I died?

No.

I had a greater mission. I was being called to teach and empower people who have experienced a life trauma to discover the gifts in their challenges and use them as a foundation for a new life. By then, my commitment to share these lessons had become so strong that it overpowered saying "yes" to the Olympics.

To learn more about Holly Eburne, visit www.expertauthorpublishing.com/cob.

No More Shame on You!
Kit Furey, JD, CHt, CEHP

"Is it normal," a graduate student asked in a small voice, "to feel stupid after getting an edited manuscript back?" This question posed instantly touched my heart when I read it recently in an article by Rachel Toor.[1] His context for feeling shame was writing; however, shame limits joy for every human, in some context, at some time. And just what is shame? Well, embarrassment is about something we've done. But shame and humiliation call forth a question about who we are at our core.

I flashed to the research of Dr. Brené Brown.[2] She concludes that shame is the fear of disconnection. Shame drives that bone-chilling inner question, "Is there something about me that if other people know it or see it, I won't be worthy of connection?" And the real problem with this silent epidemic, she says, is that in our culture shame lurks in the dark, beneath the surface of the topics most people are willing to talk about.

We're socialized not to discuss shame. And that's precisely how "shame" keeps its sneaky tendrils of limitation hooked in our unconscious mental and

---

1   "Shame in Academic Writing," The Chronicle of Higher Education, August 3, 2011, http://chronicle.com/article/Shame-In-Academic-Writing/128483

2   Brown, Brené, PhD., LMSW. I Thought It Was Just Me (but it isn't): Telling the Truth About Perfectionism, Inadequacy and Power. New York: Gotham Books, 2008, and her funny, brilliant 20-minute presentation, "The Power of Vulnerability", http://www.ted.com/talks/lang/eng/brene_brown_on_vulnerability.html

emotional programming. Shame is like a vigilant gatekeeper, magnifying the dangers of being vulnerable, shielding us from authentic connection, cautioning each of us to protect the "persona," that identity we've so carefully developed. Shame assures us that clinging to a desire to be perfect is better than surrendering to the imperfection that is our divine perfection just as we are.

Believe me, I'm not just sharing Brown's theory here. I've lived it. There've been times in my life when shame has sucked the very wind out of my sails. But nothing has been like my most recent experience. I'm just beginning to emerge from a "dark night of the soul." I've felt gripped and spun hard by my inner turmoil. I've leaned to the point of toppling on a friend or two, questioned 57 (at least) assumptions about my values, my capabilities, my Purpose. I've cried a lot even though I'm not a "crier." I have been in a financial panic because business ideas that should have been aces didn't go anywhere, capsized time and again when I should have been experiencing smooth sailing and a "return on my investment." I've felt the repercussions of all that in several significant business and personal relationships, and most of all in my relationship with myself.

Beyond embarrassment, I've been doing an excruciating dance with shame and humiliation. Source (a word I use to mean God, the Universe, the Creator) asked me a few months ago to help dissolve shame from collective consciousness. (Have you ever been called to do something you felt was too big? This was one of those times for me.) And apparently it's been important for me to consciously feel shame in my very bones and cells in order to complete this assignment. I've tried six ways from Sunday to avoid what I've gone through, to no avail. Feeling shame and surrendering to it seem to be what I'm being called to do. My "dark night of the soul" has been "research", which as the saying goes "if it doesn't crush you will make you stronger."

The terror, the panic, the razor's edge that split me in two was being called to trust that, in each moment, "everything is perfect" vs. do what a "responsible human being does," which is take action. It's been hard to sit here and know that this is part of a process and everything will work itself out. I've given my word to people that I would pay them money by particular dates. When I give my word I mean it. And I haven't had the funds.

I'm an Instant Breakthrough Belief and Energy Transformation Expert, trained to detect and help people shift limiting beliefs. I constantly examine my beliefs. And as I've done my own wary dance with this culprit, shame, and as I've helped my clients, here's what I've noticed: Shame flavors all three of the major categories of core limiting beliefs in the model of human experience I use. In the model I use, "global" categories of core limiting beliefs cluster around (1) abandonment and betrayal vs. our hard-wired longing for connection, (2) undeserving (iterations of "am I enough?") vs. significance and self-worth, and (3) core questions of trust, safety, surrender and discernment. Shame is so pervasive it oozes through all the categories of limiting beliefs. And its sneakiness is how it maintains its grip.

I'm nothing if not tenacious, to the point of calling myself a pattern detective. I'm thorough and creative. What I was dealing with was elusive and slippery. There was something more blocking a complete release from my "dark night of the soul."

My turning point came when I knew in my bones I was facing a "something's gotta give" moment. I asked a colleague to help me. We joined hearts and I dove deep into my inner world. With my inner eye I saw a veil lifting and what I could sense but not see became visible. In the inner world I saw dark and murky energy, seeming to penetrate every cell of my body.

> *The energy lifted, like watching a gentle breeze blow away black smog.*

In that instant I chose the only moment of total surrender I've ever experienced. Out loud I summoned Source and every Archangel, Ascended and Light Being I could think of and said: "You have to help me. This is too big for me to do alone. I've done everything I know to do. You must help me. Right this minute. Now." Then I let go. Really let go. Source and my Inner Team responded. The energy lifted, like watching a gentle breeze blow away black smog.

I slept 11 hours that night. The next day in meditation I asked the question, "What was the energy that released?" And the response from Source was loud and clear: "Shame. In your cellular memories."

Now, let's move to some good news. The flip side offered by Brené Brown to experiencing shame is this: Being whole-hearted. Knowing we are worthy of love and connection. And ... breathe into this with me now ... a willingness to be vulnerable. "Vulnerability is at the core of shame and fear and struggle for worthiness, and it appears it is the birthplace of joy, of creativity, of belonging and love," says Brown.

Yes! In vulnerability, in authenticity, is the richness of claiming your true Self. In the courage to be imperfect we get connection as a result of authenticity, of letting go of who we thought we were, and the compassion to be kind to self first, and then to others.

I see how this experience forced me to champion myself in the way I've fiercely championed my children. So in this paradox of becoming my strongest by being my most vulnerable, I experienced a key transformation concept: I released preconceived notions of who I thought I was and brought my energy and focus into the present moment, fully present to my Self.

So if you're plagued, knowingly or not, by our culture's silent epidemic called shame, I offer another transformational key as an antidote to shame.

A first step, an extremely effective key to releasing shame, is self-forgiveness. Let yourself off the hook for even entertaining the core question, "Am I worthy of love and connection?" Of course you are! Let yourself off the hook for learning from mistakes because, after all, that's our human experience. Bring your energy and focus into the present moment so you can live each day to the fullest.

Self-forgiveness is no small assignment. However, it doesn't have to be hard. It doesn't have to take months and months of therapy. You don't have to be sucked into painful memories and trauma from the past. Rather, you can simply engage the phenomenal power of your subconscious to re-align and re-direct your thoughts and emotions. I'm not going to go into the neuroscience of why the subconscious is really the powerhouse, the driver behind 90% plus of the experiences and results you achieve in life. I'm not going into the studies that show the subconscious processes about 40 *billion bits* of data per second while the conscious mind can handle a mere 40 *bits* of data per second. That's a topic for another day. However, you can experience the results of your subconscious mind working for you with a complimentary guided instant breakthrough audio forgiveness session found on my website.

To learn more about Kit Furey, visit
www.expertauthorpublishing.com/cob.

I Know This Much is True
Rosemary Sneeringer

Popcorn was flowing, stashes of chocolate and bottles of beer were being consumed. Cackles of laughter were heard from freshman girls in my dorm, sitting on the hall floor, talking into the night. It was post midterm finals and the last night before Spring break.

The laughing and teasing continued when I got a ride home with a bunch of guys. Every time the song "I know this much is true," by Tears for Fears came on, they would crank if up and even sing it to me because they knew I hated that song. It made me giggle even more. I was feeling at home in my college environment, having a lot of fun and making some solid friendships.

I was happy as I closed the door to the car and walked into my house. My parents greeted me cautiously and my Dad asked me to sit at the kitchen table—they had something to tell me. My sister, 17, had been hitchhiking with another girl. They were picked up by a man—

"Oh God, did he—"

"No, nothing like that, but he was drunk and hit a tree."

Her friend was unhurt, but my sister flew through the windshield and hit the pavement. She was in a coma.

"When did this happen?"

"Last weekend," my Dad said.

"Why didn't anyone tell me?"

"It was finals—we wanted you to concentrate..."

My sister and I were very close. My mind kept searching the events over and over, thinking: if only this, if only that. Not only did I feel crushed, I felt guilty and responsible. I was one year older than Meg and more than once we'd hitchhiked home.

Seeing her in the hospital was a shock. She was breathing through a tube in her throat and her body was blown up to twice her small size. Her neck was broken.

My mother cried and cried. Words like "tragedy" and "much too young" were uttered by neighbors. Even going to the grocery store was awkward. "I'm sorry about your sister," said a guy who went to our high school. "That's okay, it's not your fault," slipped out of my mouth. What a strange custom to say "I'm sorry."

Before I went back to school, my Dad wanted us to tease my sister, get her riled up so she would "wake up." It was a last-ditch desperate effort in a time when nobody knew much about comas.

At school, a heavy weight consumed my heart and my throat. I could relate to the song "It's the end of the world. . . " because I wondered how people could just go about their business as if everything was normal. Didn't they know the world had changed forever?

Four weeks later, I got the call. I took the longest two-hour bus ride of my life. The wake was on St. Patrick's Day and I was annoyed that my namesake aunt wore shamrock pins on her jacket. Did she have to be cutesy on this of all days? The funeral was packed—so many school friends. And my Mom hung onto the casket as it was being lowered into the ground at the cemetery, calling my sister's name and telling her she loved her.

Again, my dad, broken and forlorn, sat me down and explained that politicians and businessmen thought they had power, but only the Man Upstairs really did.

When I would go home my Mom would want to visit the cemetery, but I never felt like Meg was there—I could contact her anywhere if I wanted to communicate with her. And I had a strong conviction that she was okay—more than okay. Sometimes my mom would say, "Why doesn't anyone talk about Meggie?" And when we were discussing guardian angels, she said, "Where was Meg's guardian angel?" with a sob in her voice.

Eight years later I moved to Los Angeles and sought out spiritual experts. I was told that my sister's soul had opted out early. She was accepted at the University of Rochester and was on track to become a CPA—Dad's track. Her soul decided to end this life early, because, as a guitarist, she really wanted to be a performer. She had reincarnated already as a violin prodigy. This was incredibly painful to hear when I was thinking, *How could she just go like that? What about US?*

I took channeling class for 11 years, and some people in the other classes decided to pursue mediumship—talking to people who had crossed over. The public was invited to attend. When someone contacted a relative in a session, they could feel the light and love emanating from them, and it made the grief and acceptance process so much easier. Not many people can deny having an experience.

In one case a woman's husband had been shot by drug dealers in a phone booth as he was talking on the phone with her. They had both been addicted to drugs, and when the class contacted him, the dead man said he wasn't going to be able to quit drugs as his wife had, so his soul sought another life of spiritual growth.

Years later I bought a house from a young widow with a three-year-old daughter whose husband, a roofer, had died of skin cancer. Channeling with a friend, I said, "Maybe this happened so she could be more independent," and her guide answered, "No one ever dies to benefit somebody else."

Those who have passed on are not buoyed up by your grief but by your happiness.

I was right to trust that feeling that my sister was okay. I feel that people who die are free of emotional and physical pain—they have remerged with love, connection and oneness—and are choosing their next life based on what their soul wants to experience. Death is freeing—even beautiful, and at some level we all choose it—we are not its victims. Of course those left behind feel a sense of loss, but feeling sorry for those who have died does not really help them and only adds to our grief. After all, grieving is never as long for a 94 year old as 4 year old, but both have completed their soul missions.

My belief is that those who have passed on want you to be happy and celebrate the completion of their lifetime. They are not buoyed up by your grief but by your happiness. They want the same for you and more—more love and more light and more joy in your own world, just as they are feeling, and nothing less.

To learn more about Rosemary Sneeringer, visit www.expertauthorpublishing.com/cob.

Always In Our Hearts
Karin Volo

During the most difficult time in my life, I went on a journey deep inside myself as a way to escape the bars around my physical body. I was falsely accused in a US legal case related to my conman first husband and separated from my young daughters for almost four years. While I fought for my life from within the walls of a high security jail, I also gained some incredible insights into our world and how the universe works. The experience I share here is one of the greatest lessons I learned and I hold it very near my heart. It profoundly changed the way I look at the world.

Immersed in reading to escape the negative environment, books became my best friends and helped me to maintain a sense of sanity in a surreal world. One book led to another. After hundreds of books on many topics including self-help, spiritual life, religion, quantum physics, and countless others, I began to read about life after death and near death experiences. The most fascinating books on this topic were by Dr. Brian Weiss, a well-known psychotherapist who has studied life after death through past life regressions with thousands of patients. His books opened my eyes to the possibility we don't actually die. Our form changes from our physical bodies to our spiritual essence. I had several experiences behind those bars that showed me this was true.

I'd never given much thought to life after death. Although several close family members had passed away during my life, I'd never connected with them in a way that made me feel they might still be around. The first significant incident took place during a meditation, when I was feeling very alone and afraid, tired of so many months of uncertainty. In this meditation, I suddenly felt and saw in my mind my brother, my father, and my grandfather—three very dear men in my life who had passed away—sitting around me. When they were alive, all three men were over 6'6". I was in a 10-foot by 12-foot cell. These men were sitting on a small metal bunk with me, encompassing me with one on my right and the other two on my left. Although they didn't say anything to me, I felt their strong presence and was comforted and relieved to know I wasn't really alone. After this experience, I felt protected and watched over in that dismal place.

In another meditation, the face of a short elderly Mexican woman with glasses and hair worn in a bun came to me. I somehow knew she was the grandmother of an inmate in the tank at the time. She gave me a very clear message to give to her granddaughter, Centa. I didn't know what to do with this because I didn't know this person other than her name. I put it out of my mind thinking, "This is crazy, I can't tell her this." But the next day, as I was doing my 26-pace walk back and forth across the distance of the tank, I saw Centa alone in her cell and her grandmother's image appeared in my mind again, very strongly urging me to talk to her. I figured I had nothing to lose so I did. As I gave Centa the message, she burst into tears because it was exactly what she needed to hear. I was blown away because I certainly didn't consider myself a medium.

These experiences prepared me for the hardest time I ever had while incarcerated. My sister was diagnosed with cancer for the second time in her life while I was still sitting in jail after two and a half years. She went through six months of treatment and was given a clean bill of health—the cancer was gone. However, a month later, she fainted, went into a coma and then died the day before Christmas. It was a complete shock to me and to my entire family. Apparently because her immune system was destroyed from all the treatment, her body couldn't handle a simple winter cold.

The true essence of who we are simply cannot die.

My daughters lost the only aunt they'd ever had, my mother lost the second of her three children, and I lost my only sister while sitting in jail on another continent. By this time, I had read many of Dr. Brian Weiss' books and had a good understanding that our souls come to have a life on this planet. As we face challenges and obstacles we grow and learn on a spiritual level. And just as water changes from ice to liquid to steam...our souls take on the physical body but return back to our Source energy when our physical body passes. The true essence of who we are simply cannot die. We just change form.

Learning this gave me the ability to look at the hell I was living in from a different perspective, understanding that on a soul level, this was happening to me for a higher purpose. This became clearer on the other side of this nightmare, when my charges were dropped and I was free to go home.

When my sister passed, I prayed for her to come and tell me WHY. She did. Her time was done and she felt she could do more good from the spiritual realm than in the physical world. She came to me, and, I learned later, to my daughters, in vivid dreams shortly after she passed. Making contact with her in this way gave us the confirmation that she was still there. . .and always would be there. Just a thought away and always in our hearts.

To learn more about Karin Volo, visit
www.expertauthorpublishing.com/cob.

Leaping into the Unknown
Shawna Craig

Although we were poor growing up, my mom managed to get me into a private school because it was her job to clean the school and the church attached to it. I helped her. We lived in a small town near Tallahassee, Florida. My mom was almost deported back to Mexico when I was very young, but was allowed to stay because she was my sole guardian. She went on to become a U.S. citizen, even owning her own home and car. I remember Mom going without so I could take packed lunches to school like the other kids. She has always been courageous and persistent. I've always felt a strong need to move forward and build on her many successes.

All through grade school, I stood out from my classmates as the only Latin girl in a room of mainly fair children. I remember safety pinning a huge skirt at my waist as I tried to conform to the school dress code. Still it wasn't enough and I was forced to replace offending items with "suitable" items from a box the teachers stocked with the most horrible things they could find at Goodwill. It was an exercise meant to demoralize. I was a curvy girl and I was punished for this. Despite this, I strove to do the right things. I was athletic, a top player on the basketball, volleyball and track teams. I sang, danced and acted. I was outgoing and curious, very much my own person, but it was a strict school and I was always being torn down.

I remember one teacher who acted as a mentor until the day I challenged her interpretation of a Bible story in class. She stuck stubbornly to the school's view and humiliated me in front of the other students. It was a stifling environment for me and being there made my soul ache. From Grade 7 through Grade 10 when I finally left, I was in tears every day. Junior and senior years were better because I was a fixture at the Florida State University film school for acting auditions, something I loved to do.

I always knew I wanted a life in the performing arts. I lived in the same place my whole life and felt I was in a rut. Because we didn't have money, my goal was to get into college and study Fine Arts. The idea of leaving the familiar behind was exciting! I took a chance, auditioning for a spot on the local college's show choir along with about 200 others and won. By this time, I had put in countless hours to earn five academic and Fine Arts scholarships. I was attending college and performing on stage. In the beginning it was great, but after a while I realized I wasn't really happy. I wondered if it was because although I had changed my situation, I was still around the same people I had always known.

I chose to move two hours further from Tallahassee to a different college in a beach town. This meant giving up some of the scholarships and their financial benefits. I was nervous but soon I was setting my own schedule, enjoying life by the seaside, and it was—nice. Shortly after, however, I felt that need for something more.

Then came my decision to move to California.

I called a friend who lived in San Diego and talked to him about my dream of acting in Hollywood and my frustration with what I was doing. He and his roommates were in the Navy, leaving for Iraq. He suggested if I moved there, I'd be in California with a place to stay and time to figure things out. Quitting college after only two years would mean giving up my scholarships, the security of a college degree and its benefits in the job market. I worked so hard to get to where I was. If I went to San Diego, I wouldn't have school or a place to work. My friend wouldn't even be there to show me around. I would be dropping everything to follow my heart. It would be the first time I had done anything that big and a huge leap into the unknown. I decided to do it.

I always had several jobs at once and at the time was working in retail, waitressing and bartending at two locations. I started rolling the quarters from my change while waitressing and bartending and put them in a shoebox under my bed. I was on a mission! I saved for about two months. One day, in an almost random way, I thought, "I'm moving to California." I cashed out my quarters, which weighed about 25 pounds, and found I had $500 for travel money to get there. I also had about $2000 in the bank. I packed my car and drove to San Diego, arriving 36 hours later. I cut the three-day drive in half because I didn't want anything—a car problem, natural disaster, or a change of mind—to interfere with my now-desperate need to get to California. It was the most terrifying experience of my life, but it was also a defining moment in my life and the best decision I ever made.

My experiences have given me the ability and confidence to take leaps into new territory.

I enjoyed getting to know San Diego and made some very good friends. Three years later, when I decided it was time to move to Los Angeles, my enthusiasm convinced one of my friends to take this big step with me. I had even less money than when I initially moved to California, but I felt in my heart this risk would pay off. The house we found to live in was full of friendly roommates, even if we did have to wear earplugs to sleep with the constant pool party going on! I just felt so happy to be making my dreams come true.

My experiences have given me the ability and confidence to take leaps into new territory. Sometimes the leaps into the unknown are smaller and sometimes they are bigger. They all take courage because you must often leave the familiar behind and take a risk. I've always had goals, but these days I have a *list* of goals that change—I check things off and add new things constantly. In fact, I now accept that every two or three years it's natural for me to re-evaluate and reassess my life. I'm not a complacent person—I feed on constant challenge. I think the difficult memories from my grade school days, my mom's persistence, and the knowledge that many people from those small towns are still content in not growing and moving forward, all help motivate me to keep following my heart.

When I moved to Los Angeles a few years ago, I soon met my husband, Lorenzo Lamas, at the gym. I always said I'd never get married! I couldn't have predicted the fulfillment and pleasure I get being married with six stepchildren, but now I wouldn't have it any other way. The last few years, I've been an egg donor at a fertility agency and this experience has had very real rewards—it's a contrast to the superficiality you can find at times in Hollywood. I now work at the clinic and I'm also continuing my acting career. I look forward to taking more leaps into the unknown. I've come so far on this amazing journey and I still have so far to go.

To learn more about Shawna Craig, visit www.expertauthorpublishing.com/cob.

Shifting Gears
J.F. Parkinson

Cruising through my 20's, sporting the ultimate in "cool"—Roy Orbison shades; Led Zeppelin blaring; hair flying on a mid-winter breeze—accessorized by one tonne of steel on wheels. Now that's what I call "a ticket to ride."

Picture it ... an '85 Nissan Pulsar—She was a beauty—jet black; grey stripes; five speed, AM/FM cassette.

Together, we were one.

Driving to work one day, at a speed suitable to the rainy weather, my Pulsar and I were just gearing down to head for the off ramp. Suddenly, the engine revs went up and the wheel revs went down.

We coasted off to the side and shut down all engines. My cardiac muscle shifted into aerobic high gear.

When my hands stopped shaking, I tried turning the key. The engine sounded funky alright, but I was insistent that at some point the motor would catch and my beauty would ignite.

Nope.

It was toast.

I loved that car and it let me down ... in the rain ... in the muck ... and in the dark. This was to be the first of my many encounters with the "tow truck."

No matter how hard you try to prepare for life's little catastrophes, it never helps. It took $1,500.00 plus, to get that little sucker out of the mechanic's hands and back into mine. We managed to break the timing chain and wipe out three out of four valves (not a bad percentage).

Unfortunately, that car never forgave me either. Upon occasion after that, and only when I was driving, it would hack, it would cough, it would sputter and it would die. My mechanic had it for two weeks, took it everywhere—worked like a gem.

I picked it up, drove out of the lot and about a half mile down the road it recognized my foot. One cough and it quit.

I don't think anyone ever believed me, except maybe the guy who bought it.

Next!

It was a 1984 Pulsar, white, with red stripes—A peppy little five-speed that only took a couple of hundred bucks to pass the medical. Off we went. Getting from point "A" to point "B" was a breeze—As long as I didn't have to back up.

It was tough getting it into reverse, regardless of how hard I would stomp on the clutch.

I had to look for "drive though" parking spots. If I couldn't find one, I had to jam the shifter into reverse when the car was still warm. That year I built up quite a bit of strength and muscle tone in my right arm, and my left leg. The calluses on my hand were just a bonus.

I stopped every morning at the donut shop to get a medium coffee, double cream, regular sugar; ok and an apple fritter. So I pulled the heap into a space not really suited for it, but it had to do. Reefing it into reverse, I got out and carried on across the parking lot. Somebody honked and I turned to see who—someone was frantically waving at me and motioning in the direction from whence I had just come.

I casually glanced back.

Here comes my car—headed for the curb that was BEHIND the car parked in front of it.

Bionic woman engaged and I jumped in front of my moving car, slowed it to a crawl, got in, fired it up, put it back into the same spot, jammed it into reverse and applied the PARKING BRAKE—then nonchalantly went off in search of caffeine.

That one had to go.

The descent into car hell was now in full gear.

Next!

The 1988 Corsica was a four door "family" sedan—white, with red interior and a radio with no audible reception capabilities. But it was a five-speed and I was desperate.

Sold.

It had to be towed within 12 hours of the change of ownership—something about a clutch switch. Following that, and after I put in a decent AM/FM cassette deck, we co-habited quite nicely for the next two months.

It was the coldest day of the year, and not much of a surprise when it wouldn't start.

Boosted it.

Nope.

I plugged in the block heater which I had just found.

Nope.

The weather warmed, but the cylinder head just didn't have any brains left. I had to fix or scrap. I may as well have set fire to another 1,500 bucks.

I fixed it.

It was about that time that my dad was nosing around the car lots looking for something a bit newer than what he had. He found one. We now had twins.

Station wagons, that is.

My first six-cylinder ... my first automatic and my second family sedan.

I learned the hard way that it didn't stop on a dime like the others. I put that vehicle through more intersections on yellow lights trying to stop—clutch and brake feet to the floor ... and I kept forgetting about that "park" thing. The key wouldn't turn if it wasn't in park, and putting it in PARK without using the brake first was, well, not recommended. Every time I tried to clean the windshield, the high beams came on. It took a while to get used to, but I managed—all the while staying incognito to some extent with shades.

I realize the more we enjoy and laugh in the face of change, the easier it becomes.

I think the whole station wagon issue hit home when one of the guys I worked with asked, "Do you have kids?"

"No. Why?"

"I thought I saw you getting out of a station wagon."

As I look back and laugh now, I realize that life is merely the constant shifting of gears—and the more we enjoy and laugh in the face of change, the easier it becomes. I must say, that in spite of the trials and tribulations, I loved every single one of those cars—especially the last one. Thanks Dad.

To learn more about J.F. Parkinson, visit
www.expertauthorpublishing.com/cob.

Inspiration Versus Desperation
Nikkea Devida

Every day when I woke up, I promised myself that "today would be different." But before noon, I found myself obsessing about food and planning my next binge. Thoughts of food and my body weight occupied over 90% of my waking hours. Every day, an average of two to six times per day, for 13 years, I suffered with an eating disorder, bulimia.

For most of my life, it was a constant effort and struggle to overcome the numerous negative and traumatic situations I had encountered since childhood. And frankly, I'm proud to say I developed some pretty good skills over the years. Instead of reacting to or being a victim of my circumstances, I learned to respond to them.

Part of my growth path has been developing the perspective to see the silver lining and benefit out of the challenges I've experienced in my life and how they've supported my ability to emerge stronger, like the Phoenix rising from the ashes.

Overall, I think having this point of view has been healthy and beneficial for me so that I stay out of "victim" mentality and I take personal responsibility for my life's circumstances. For years, I valued this as a way to continually learn, grow and evolve.

As a competitive athlete and even an officer in the Air Force, I really took to heart messages like:

"No pain, no gain."

"What doesn't kill you makes you stronger."
"It [adversity and challenge] builds character."
And based on that criteria, I felt like I had plenty of character, because nothing in my life came easily. I survived a physically, emotionally, and violently abusive childhood. I overcame enormous temptations as a young teen to break the cycle and pursue the disciplines of academics and athletics instead of drugs and alcohol. To escape the pain of my family life, I immersed myself in athletics and schoolwork and was a straight-A student. Then, I endured and tapped into every bit of strength I had to make it through and graduate from the United States Air Force Academy ... especially as a woman. I struggled to overcome bulimia. I was even hospitalized for four months and was medically discharged from the Air Force back in 1990, right in the middle of a nationwide economic and real estate crisis.

It was a constant struggle to just pay the bills and get by financially.

I believed that everything in my life worth having, was worth struggling and fighting for. So I wore all the struggles that I'd overcome as a badge of honor.

Until one day, in one moment, everything changed.

I was sitting in a church service one Sunday when I heard my minister, Reverend Sue, give her Sunday sermon. And her words that day changed the course of my life.

She said, "A lot of people who are interested in personal growth and development really value overcoming challenges and growing through our experiences. But if you value overcoming challenges and you always have to learn through struggle—what will you always attract? More challenges and struggle, right? And what happens when you get really good at overcoming challenges and struggles? What do you naturally have to get more of? Bigger and better challenges and struggles, right? Do you see the problem here?" She said "Wouldn't it be better if you could learn and grow through **inspiration** versus **desperation**?"

I had to let those words sink in. After all, my life up until that point was all about learning and growing by overcoming my life's challenges. Before Reverend Sue said those words, it literally hadn't occurred to me that it could be any other way.

When I heard those words, they totally shifted my perspective and changed my life forever. So using some of my own belief change tools, I literally sat right there in that church pew and turned that sermon into a positive belief statement and programmed that belief into my subconscious right away.

"I learn, grow, and evolve through inspiration versus desperation."

I wanted THAT belief to be my new default program in my subconscious.

What that belief now allows me to do is see the vision of what I want to achieve in my life, and move toward it quickly without all the struggle, fight and drama.

I've now learned that when I'm not following my divine path or higher knowing, the Universe/God sends me a message in a quiet whisper. If I don't hear the whisper, the message will come with a gentle tap on the shoulder. If I don't get the tap, I'll get a push or a slap to get my attention. If I still don't get it (yes, it happens!), I'll get a 2 X 4 board across my forehead to knock me on my butt.

So, now, **I do my best to listen to the message when it comes in a whisper (inspiration), so I can avoid the 2 X 4 across my forehead (desperation).** As a result of listening more and more to the whispers over the past eight plus years, my path has been a lot easier, a lot faster, and I now achieve my goals without nearly as much struggle.

For example, this summer, I was attending an event and I heard a speaker who inspired me to write a song as a fundraiser for women veterans. I acted on that inspiration and immediately met several people who could assist me. The inspiration came and I wrote the lyrics. Within a week of that, I "coincidentally" met the perfect people to help me with the arrangement and production of the song, who "coincidentally" were also guests on a radio station on Veteran's Day. I was also invited to be a guest on the show representing women veteran's issues to nearly one million listeners. I couldn't have planned all those synchronicities. They resulted from taking inspired action on the whisper.

Now, that doesn't mean I don't have to work to get what I want. I do. But I see the results of my work more directly, and I'll take inspired action on a hunch or whisper (even if it seems crazy) and I'll get to my goal even faster ... sometimes even seemingly magically.

As a result, I don't get nearly as many setbacks, crises, or dramas, etc. as I used to. And when I do get one, I really take it as an opportunity to sit back and deeply reflect on what the heck is going on, and get back in touch with the inspiration.

*I think change is inevitable,
but that struggle is optional.*

Once I get that inspiration, I gratefully take action and follow through with it. I like the idea of learning and growing through divine guidance and inspiration versus desperation. The way I figure it, inspiration equals pleasure, and desperation equals pain and struggle. I think change is inevitable, but that struggle is optional. My goal is to continually get better to listen to the whisper earlier to avoid the 2 X 4!

I think the 2 X 4's have led me to my life's work. But I know that the whispers are now leading me to my destiny.

*To learn more about Nikkea Devida, visit
www.expertauthorpublishing.com/cob.*

Stealing An Idea
Anne Briggs Buzzini

My jaw dropped open and I stared at Dr. Clum, President of Life Chiropractic College West as he continued to speak to the assembled prospective students. I was unaware that my internal universe had changed in a moment. I was going to be a chiropractor. I had one of those astonishingly spellbinding aha moments as my body felt vitalized, my fingertips buzzed with energy, my thoughts connected at light-speed; even the light in the auditorium seemed different. Now I understood the reports about these moments of the heavens opening and angels singing. I got it.

Wait a minute, I thought. *Until two years ago I had been scared silly of those bonecrackers—and now I'm going to go into massive debt to become one?*

Every atom of my body and particle of my being said, "Yes, this is the next step on your path."

I should have known. Any time I say "never" to anything that is exactly what manifests somewhere down the line. I should qualify that: any time I have a visceral fear reaction, a pulling away from something when there is no rational reason to fear it (like driving in San Francisco with a stick shift or living in Pocatello) that's when I know that is absolutely where I need to go.

The first time I saw a chiropractic adjustment, I was about 14 years old and accompanied my friend to her appointment. The doctor told her to lie on her side, bent her knee up to her waist and sort of fell on her. I remember my friend laughing at the horrified look on my face as I inched toward the door. Then he told her to lie on her back and did something to her neck—as if he was trying to yank it off. My friend sat up and thanked the doctor, telling him it felt much better, but I didn't see how that was possible.

Apparently, my reaction to the experience at home was intense. My mother had been secretly seeing a chiropractor since she was seven and she didn't tell me until I was graduating.

After that, any time I heard someone mention chiropractic, I would get cold shivers down my spine. I asked many people how they could stand to have someone do that to them. I received a wide variety of replies but none that really satisfied me. The terms used for it—bonecrunchers, backcrackers, etc.—did nothing to inspire my confidence in them either. I decided everything works for some subset of the population and left it at that.

My first experience on a chiropractor's table was after being sick for two weeks and continuing to feel like passing out and vomiting if I stood up. My boyfriend decided it was time to see if a chiropractor friend of his could help. I protested, but he picked me up and put me in the car while reassuring me this miracle worker wouldn't hurt me. This buoyant doctor in sneakers, shorts, and a baseball hat performed what he called a "low-force adjustment" using his hands and a table with parts that popped up and dropped about an inch and made odd hydraulic noises. I got off the table after several of these adjustments and told him that was the strangest experience I had ever had in any health practitioner's office. He laughed. Half an hour later I was ready for dinner and a movie.

Several other atypical experiences led me back to his office—including a failed attempt at using allopathic medicine to treat a psychologically-induced asthma attack after my grandmother died—before I mentioned to him I had ongoing neck pain from a decade of playing the viola.

Eventually, a change in boyfriends among the twists of my life path led me to sitting in the auditorium listening to Dr. Clum, thinking I was there to lend moral support as my boyfriend chose which school he would attend for his own education. My job as an accountant at a gold mine had become less and less rewarding. My study of energy work was pulling me in another direction—I wanted to help people and explore the unseen realms.

The knowingness that change was coming in my own career had grown in the past few months, but my rational mind had said to wait until the boyfriend had chosen his school and decide from there. With this new epiphany ringing in my head, I turned and asked, "Mind if I steal your idea?"

"What? His expression reflected the shock I expected to see on my own.

"I want to go to school here." The words almost corrected themselves. "I am going to school here."

Once the decision was made, I had to move fast. In order to start at the same time as my boyfriend, I had to take two years of science prerequisites in six months, along with a couple of classes I had missed in my first set of degrees. Ironically, in my undergraduate degrees in accounting and computer information systems, I had assiduously avoided the sciences with labs, as they meant extra time and work for no credit. This required me to drive 1,200 miles round trip to San Jose, California to attend weekend classes and return home to attend class at the community college on Monday evening, while working four ten-hour days. After six months of this brutal schedule, it was over and time to start school. Four years later, I graduated Summa Cum Laude. That was 14 years ago.

Fear blocks us from our true potential.

By being willing to change that one belief, I have changed my whole life. Now I help others change their beliefs about chiropractic, about healing and about themselves. Fear is one of the greatest beliefs blocking us from our true potential. Now that I have accomplished this, I know that conquering a fear is taking me not into darkness, but into expansion, joy and life.

To learn more about Anne Buzzini, visit www.expertauthorpublishing.com/cob.

'Til Death Do Us Part
Amethyst Wyldfyre

I grew up like most little girls with the dream planted in me that someday my "handsome prince" would arrive, kiss my ruby red lips, awaken my heart and carry me off to live "Happily Ever After." This dream was nourished by my mother in the extreme. When I was only 14 she picked out the fabric for my wedding dress and stored it in my "Hope Chest" along with various other items I'd be needing so that I could properly entertain my future husband.

I remember when I thought I was getting married the first time. My college boyfriend traveled all the way from Pennsylvania to New Hampshire to ask for my hand in marriage. This of course excited my mother to no end. In the days before cell phones, she managed to track me down and have me emergency paged on the intercom at a restaurant where I was having fun with friends: I was to call her right away. I thought someone had died. But no, it was the boyfriend freshly arrived from his road trip with the little ring nestled in his front pants pocket. After spending a weekend alone together I had a deep inner knowing that my life with him would end up like my parents—a constant battleground filled with dysfunction. I could see the writing on the wall— I'd be his "servant" washing his laundry, doing his dishes and waiting on him hand and foot and he'd be the "master of the house" to be obeyed without question because he was the man. Thankfully at 18 I was somehow strong enough to say no to that one.

My next "frog" was a real dangerous one. Together we went down the path of serious drug abuse—he was a dealer and I was the "mule." After two years of living together, we made plans to marry, and once again my mom was activated into "let's get ready for the big day" mode. We had the fabric made into a lovely dress—ivory, trimmed with a wide band of Belgian Lace. The date was set—mid-May 1985. Three weeks before the wedding I looked in the mirror and knew once again I had to get out. This wasn't the one for me, and, in fact, if I didn't leave immediately I was going to end up dead.

Not one to quit on the "dream" of the handsome prince, my next long-term relationship took me to the other end of the spectrum. I moved in with Mr. Tall Dark and Handsome, a police officer studying to become an attorney. He taught me a lot—appreciating fine wines and learning how to use a pistol were part of this romance. Things were great—maybe this was "the ONE." Until the "Dark" part of Mr. Tall Dark and Handsome showed itself, first in the form of a little shove... "Surely that was a mistake," I told myself. Unfortunately it wasn't. Finally, when the gun went into my face and I was held up against the wall for something to do with not doing the laundry correctly, it was clear as day that Mr. Right was Mr. Oh SO WRONG. The dress stayed in the Hope Chest.

Eventually I moved in with another man—this one didn't seem too bad. He had a big family, he didn't drink, smoke or do drugs. He was over all that. He had a decent job and wanted a home. We lived together for a year and a half, bought a house together, and decided to go for it. I wanted a baby, my biological clock was ticking LOUDLY, and it was time. There were signs though, right from the get-go, that my husband-to-be had some mental health issues, although he was medicated and it was mostly under control. He had a little habit of shoplifting and flying into uncontrollable rages every now and again. When he asked me to marry him the first time I actually said no because "We don't share the same values." Eventually, because I believed I wasn't getting any younger and I didn't feel like I had the time to start AGAIN to find Mr. Right, I decided to compromise, dig that 10-year-old dress out of the Hope Chest and make my way down the aisle, contracting to be with him "til death do us part." I knew I was settling and I believed that I could make it work, I could tolerate his flaws and maybe after we married there was a possibility for "Happily Ever After" to actually come to fruition. NOT ...

Fast-forward seven years. We have a beautiful son and a LOT of problems. I "walk on eggshells" almost all the time. The occasional RAGE is now a regular occurrence. Fear, anxiety, unhappiness and the daily drama of living with someone who is disturbed, being the breadwinner of the family and mothering fulltime are taking their toll. But I had that contract—I had made an agreement—I entered into this relationship with full awareness that I was compromising, and I believed that when I made that contract I made it FOR LIFE.

Love doesn't ask you to suffer—ever.

The MIRACLE occurred for me when somehow one day Marianne Williamson's *A Return to Love* made its way into my hands. I was PRAYING of all things for help from a God I didn't know and had no relationship with to give me the serenity to accept and honor this commitment. Thank GOD for Marianne. Her words of wisdom, personal experiences and stories about leaving bad relationships were so resonant with my own. For the first time ever in my life the thought occurred to me that I actually had a HIGHER commitment—that the most IMPORTANT CONTRACT I had was with myself and Spirit, and that LOVE doesn't ask you to suffer—ever. I changed one belief: the belief that I had to stay in my marriage "til DEATH do us part," the belief that I actually had to DIE a physical death before the bond of marriage, the commitment and contract could be broken. The day I decided to end our marriage—9/9/01—was the day I "died" to that relationship. It was also the day that I was reborn. And once that one belief changed, the realization came that I had the power to change ALL the beliefs that weren't working for me anymore!

Changing the "waiting for Mr. Right, Handsome Prince, Happily Ever After" belief took me a while longer. It wasn't until April of 2010, after a second marriage and divorce, I finally came to peace ending the fairy tale search for the "other half' and falling in love with myself. Now I understand the only way to right relationship was going deep into the core of my own being, surfacing and healing all that no longer serves: beliefs, habits, patterns of behavior, and sometimes people, circumstances or environments. I have discovered the gift of knowing who I REALLY am at my own core. I have come to understand and know my value and I have realized that the only way to true happiness is by getting clear on my OWN desires rather than trying to fit myself into what other people believe is the right way for me to be. I now take inspired action towards fulfilling those desires myself rather than expecting others to make that happen for me. My path has taken me to Spirit—not the "God" of my childhood, that big white bearded judgmental man on a chair up in the heavens—but the true Source of all that is, was and ever will be. My connection to my Source has been restored and I can truly say that I am fully alive and celebrating myself and the gifts that I am here to manifest in the world. For so long I wandered. Finally I am at home.

To learn more about Amethyst Wyldfyre, visit www.expertauthorpublishing.com/cob.

Any Body Can Change The World!
Ann Taylor

I can still recall how much it hurt when I started school at five years old and found I was immediately and relentlessly picked on because I was overweight. There was no relief when I went home, because my family was very unkind about this issue—in fact, in many ways they caused the majority of the trauma I experienced. I struggled until I discovered boys at age 12. Finally the weight came off and stayed off for a while! Hurray for hormones!

Since then, I have fluctuated between a size six and a size 16, never feeling truly comfortable or satisfied with the way I looked unless I was that "magic" size six.

Over the years, I worked hard to excel in all areas of my life, despite ups and downs with my weight and dysfunctional family issues. I was employed for over a decade as a stockbroker and then as a VP of a Fortune 500 company, but I left that industry when I was strongly guided by God, going on a long journey to prepare me for my life's mission and purpose.

I became aware of the incredible healing ability that I have when I was just turning 50. I realized I had been blessed with a gift for healing those around me struggling with emotional and psychological wounds and issues. A new career was born. Seventeen years later, this gift is my whole life, and because of it my connection to God is incredibly strong.

As I developed my abilities and continued to do healing work with more and more people, sometimes hundreds and thousands at a time over phone and Internet teleseminars, I discovered that I also could help people overcome weight issues. Not only could I eliminate addiction to food, and beliefs such as "food is love," I could empower people to lose weight and keep it off.

But while I was helping people change their lives in profound ways, I was hiding a secret. No matter what healing work I did on myself, I couldn't take off the weight I had gained in the last five years. It was unusual for me to be in this situation—usually I could fix things for myself too! I tried everything I could think of, working out, even hiring a personal trainer, but nothing helped. I knew that everything happened for a reason, I just wasn't sure what it was—yet.

More recently, I began praying to God and doing some inner work on myself in order to attain something I wanted very badly: to make friends with business-savvy people who are doing amazing work on this planet. But I kept putting off my first steps. How could I go out there and make a difference when I wasn't a physical representation of the miracles I was creating in other people's lives? I worried what other people would think of me. I passed up opportunities where I might connect with those peers I so wanted to befriend because I didn't want to get out of the house until I lost the weight.

The feeling of self acceptance was like a balm.

It took time, along with support and encouragement from people in my life, but I finally let this limiting belief go. Those closest to me kept saying things like "You're fine, " "This is the only thing that's holding you back," and "You're beautiful just the way you are and the only one who doesn't think so is you" and finally something clicked. I realized that I don't have to be a size six to get out there in the public eye and make a big difference in other people's lives. The feeling of self-acceptance was like a balm and very empowering. I realized I could experience self-acceptance no matter what my size or weight. I immediately felt a renewed vigor and excitement for life.

I started to experience some things in a very different way than I had before. In the past, saying I disliked trying on clothes would be putting it mildly. When I went clothes shopping it would seem like I had to hold my breath just to get through the horrifying ordeal. After I let go of my limiting belief about size, I did something that was a first for me. I went out to a fashionable boutique, connected with an exceptionally nice saleswoman, and then actually had fun trying on and getting some great new clothes. I was fine with the vision in the mirror. What a change to feel calm and not rush out of the store!

I couldn't wait to put myself out there and make some new connections.

When a colleague of mine said she wanted to fly in with her crew to video me, I gave a resounding "YES!" after deciding that I wasn't going to let this hold me back ever again. I loved the entire experience of being filmed and found a new passion for being in front of the camera. I was so glad my new mindset allowed me to take advantage of this opportunity!

Then, an email arrived in my inbox describing a two-day event in San Diego put on by a mentor I'd been following for quite some time. I immediately knew I had to go and made my reservations. If I had let my weight hold me back I would have never flown from Asheville, North Carolina all the way to California to attend what turned out to be a remarkable offering!

I walked into the crowded room and immediately a fabulous feeling came over me. I sensed many of these people could be friends who would really support me, friends who could meet me where I was, friends who I could say things to and they would understand immediately. After spending most of my life being the person others looked to for support, I knew with the people here it would be a two-way street. It would be a relationship of mutual trust and someone would be in my court. This was exactly what I had hoped and prayed for, and I was so blown away that tears came to my eyes.

The experience changed my life. I felt fine around everybody, and I wasn't self-conscious at all. The theme running through the people I met was genuine warmth and caring combined with wanting to be of service. It seemed that any time I sat down, I was making wonderful instant connections with amazing people who were leading the kind of lives that inspire others. I felt inspired too.

I have been so fortunate to be a naturally resilient person. I've snapped back from more adversity than any individual should experience in one lifetime. I believe that I chose this life, and a lot of what I've experienced, so that I could be of service to humanity with the healing gift I have been blessed with. And yet—I almost let my weight issue keep me from experiencing the life of my dreams.

To learn more about Ann Taylor, visit
www.expertauthorpublishing.com/cob.

Meanings, Not Experiences, Create Our Reality
Irena O'Brien, Ph.D., ACMC

I've always felt that there was something wrong with me. For most of my life, I've kept to myself. I avoided people because I was afraid they would see what was wrong with me. I dressed in gray so people wouldn't notice me. I lived in a constant state of anxiety. Every time I said or did anything, I wondered if it was the right thing. So I learned not to speak much, because I was never sure that what I wanted to say was appropriate. I was afraid of meeting new people. I was so afraid of making a mistake that it took way too long to make a decision, even a small decision like picking a restaurant.

For me to feel good enough, I could not make a mistake—I had to be perfect. I watched people's faces to gauge their reaction to me. If their reaction wasn't overtly positive, I assumed I said or did something wrong. I compared myself to others and always came up short. I remember at 12 years old wanting to become a nun because all decisions would be made for me and I would always know what to do.

I was in a straightjacket: my life was about watching myself constantly so I wouldn't make a mistake. If I did make a mistake, I would dwell on it for days. And if I did something well, I would say that it was nothing; if I could do it, anyone could. I was so unhappy as a child that I have very few childhood memories.

As an adult, I've interpreted legitimate clarification questions as personal judgments. I've abandoned careers because I felt I wasn't good enough. I've entered into relationships where I looked to the other for clues on how I should act.

One thing I did excel at was academics. I excelled because I thought that being really good at something would make me feel better about myself. Finally, I'd know I was good enough. So I graduated from university at age 20 and became a chartered accountant at 22. When I joined my accountancy firm, for many years I was the youngest member and one of very few women. I finally became a tax accountant, and when I left, my manager told me that he had never seen someone interpret tax law as well as I could. I replied that it was nothing. It didn't make me feel any better about myself.

I thought that if I got a Ph.D., the ultimate degree, I would finally feel okay. But even though I graduated with a 4.0 GPA and obtained every scholarship I applied for, it didn't change how I felt about myself at all. I still felt that there was something wrong with me.

Finally, my feelings about myself became unbearable and I started therapy. I spent 10 years in therapy. I accepted intellectually that there was nothing wrong with me, but I still didn't feel right.

Then it hit me in a Landmark Forum five years ago—a memory flashed of me standing in a hospital garden, waving goodbye to my parents. There were no other memories, but kinesthetically I felt the panic, the despair and the frozen fight-or-flight response. I never brought it up in therapy because I thought it had no effect on me. At two years old, I was hospitalized for two weeks with a life-threatening intestinal condition. What a huge relief it was to realize the impact this event had on my life. My two-year-old self believed my parents abandoned me because I wasn't good enough, but I had no conscious awareness of this belief.

When I shared this with my mother, she said this explained why she could never connect with me the way she connected with my sisters and my brother. I always pushed her away, and no matter how hard she tried, I stayed distant. My fear of people and my perfectionism began from that incident. My whole life I was afraid of being abandoned again.

> *I understood intellectually I didn't have to be perfect, but still panicked when I made a mistake.*

In 2009, I started working on changing the belief that I had to be perfect, as well as my fear of abandonment. Although I did understand intellectually that I didn't have to be perfect to be all right, that a mistake was not the end of the world and that there was no reason to fear people, I still panicked when I made a mistake—but not all mistakes, only those that could disappoint other people, and I still had a fight-or-flight response when meeting new people.

Finally, last summer I discovered I was in a "loop" at a Neuro-semantic Trainers Training event. My beliefs went like this: If I wasn't perfect, I was flawed, I was worthless. If I was worthless, I would be rejected. If I was rejected, that proved that I was worthless. No wonder working on my beliefs separately was not working! It was a huge aha moment for me, right there in front of everyone!

How has my life changed since then? I used to live with an underlying level of anxiety that was unspecified but always there. I now have peace of mind most days. When I am anxious, the source is usually something specific, and when I deal with it, the anxiety is gone. Since then, I have made great strides.

Starting my own business took me out of my comfort zone. I had to stop hiding and allow people see me as I am. Now, instead of hiding I am actually approaching people! I'm still not comfortable in a room with hundreds of people, but I do well one-on-one now and I'm fine in a room with 20 people. When I meet new acquaintances, I become present in the moment, remember their names, and enjoy the encounter, instead of being in my head interpreting every look and gesture for clues about what they think of me.

I even rejoined a tennis club I'd joined twice before. I let the membership lapse without ever setting foot in the building. I was immobilized with anxiety just thinking about this whole contingent of people I didn't know, wondering how I was going to talk to them, thinking they wouldn't like me. Now in my third year, I walk into the building knowing I have friends there.

The biggest change I notice is that I am able to network and speak on behalf of my business. I go to networking events regularly and always strike up several conversations. I realize that school was my way to hide, working on my Ph.D. I was alone and in my head all the time. When I did my postdoctoral, I knew every person in the room and I still froze—what a disaster! Recently I spoke in front of 30 people. Sure, I was nervous, but I dealt with it differently. Months before, I practiced consciously changing my fearful thoughts and made a decision not to tell anyone how nervous I was so I wouldn't increase the anxiety. I was antsy when I got up in front of the room, but I was able to relax when I focused on the participants listening to and understanding my message, rather than being fixated on how well I was delivering my speech. I was so in the moment that time seemed to fly, and at the end I saw people leaning forward with interest and clapping for me. That felt great, but even better was feeling the unwavering love and acceptance I had for myself, no matter how the speech went.

To learn more about Irena O'Brien, visit www.expertauthorpublishing.com/cob.

I Chose To Live
Kasia Rachfall

Imagine a woman sobbing on the floor in the middle of the night as a winter storm rages outside. Her body trembles with the force of her tears while her husband sleeps, exhausted from working 20-hour days. Her babies, too, sleep peacefully, despite her endless yelling throughout the day.

That was my experience in 2004 after my second child was born. My post-partum depression was running wild and my world was collapsing. Over and over again, the thoughts circled: I'm worthless; I'm a horrible mother; *I don't deserve to live.*

I felt wretched and alone, and I did not think I was strong enough to carry on one more day. We were broke. I was hormonal, stressed, and depressed. I saw no way out. I admit I contemplated suicide.

In that dark moment, I felt a tiny sliver of curiosity and tenacity. It was so small that I can't even call it a light. It was more of a fleeting feeling that flickered like a distant candle somewhere in a dark forest. Yet I knew unmistakably it was there—and this feeling wanted acknowledgement. It's almost as if it said, "Don't you owe it to yourself to do this? Once and for all, take charge of your life and *drive it forward* instead of being driven!"

Somewhere deep inside, at some level, I wanted a better life. And I knew I deserved better—so why did I keep convincing myself to stay stagnant and be a victim?

How had I come to this place where I actually contemplated suicide?

I was jealous of the moms who seemed to float through each day, making it look so easy! They smiled through stressful times instead of tearing their hair out or getting depressed. What did they know that I didn't?

I was resentful of the responsibilities I had chosen in my life. Driving to playgroups, squeezing in laundry, cooking, housework, yard work, even squeezing in sleep. I kept saying to myself, "It's my responsibility to do these things! I'm the mom!"

I was so driven doing it all for my family that I put myself last! I didn't have the energy to even think about going to the gym or having a night out with friends. Actually, I didn't have friends because I had driven them all away with my constant complaining and negativity. *And I blamed them for not sticking around and being there for me.*

I felt my life was passing me by and I wasn't getting to do what I'd always wanted to do. Sure, I wanted marriage, kids, a house and career. But any other dreams and goals slipped away as I assumed these responsibilities. I felt like a sacrificial lamb who had put aside her true calling to become a wife and mother.

I constantly worried that my children would grow up with low self-esteem and turn to drugs or gangs because I was a bad role model. I felt like such a failure knowing I could never raise well-adjusted, self-actualized adults when I myself was on the brink of suicide.

I had so many excuses for why I didn't take care of myself. No time, no money, no desire to attend playgroups or meet-ups with other "perfect moms." I felt selfish when I wanted some time to myself, but I also felt that no one else could do the job I did. I was walking around like a zombie, not present. And I was sick of telling myself that "someday" my life would get better. I was tired of waiting for that day. It was time to end it.

The Universe truly showed me the way that dark night. I decided to live. No matter what that looked like from then on . . . I decided to live.

I started to wonder where my excuses came from. Why did I keep using them? I realized they took the focus off of myself and my deep needs and desires buried inside. My "reward" was getting sympathy and the feeling of entitlement to complain about my life.

***That dark moment in my life
was a turning point.***

I began reading, listening, studying and learning everything I could about the mind and how we create our lives. I continue to do this even today because there is so much to know! *I kept a list of everything that worked and threw out everything that didn't. That dark moment in my life was a turning point, and I decided to devote the rest of my professional career to helping others get through their own dark nights.*

***

Fast-forward a few years and my story has completely changed. I am fulfilled. I have two amazingly resilient and beautifully confident, loving children, and a husband who is strong and supportive. I am living my life's dream and purpose. I am empowering other moms to help themselves find their own power.

I uncovered my own inner strength and balance. I learned what it means to have personal excellence and meaningful internal and external communication. I have developed my personal empowerment and self-esteem. I feel happy and I am kinder to myself and to others.

I found my key to happiness not only as a mom, but also as a human being.

I am now living a life that *I control and not a life that controls ME*. The secret key I found is so simple I was shocked.

But *I've lived the simplicity of it and it saved my life*, my marriage, and my children!

I discovered that *I hold the keys to living an empowered life in MY hands. When I took 100% responsibility for my choices, my actions and my inactions, my life changed immediately. I recognized the excuses and reasons I had for staying in my comfort zone and suffering through my current story, and my story changed!* I am now the creator of my own life.

To learn more about Kasia Rachfall, visit www.expertauthorpublishing.com/cob.

One Thought That Changed My Life Forever
Christine French

I stood in Dublin Airport, eyes glazed over, staring at my brother who had tears in his eyes. In all my 26 years, I had never seen him cry, so I knew this was big. My gaze shifted to my husband, also fighting back tears. I glanced to my sister, and she was smiling for me, yet tears welled up behind the smile. I was sad but excited at the same time. I couldn't believe this day was here. Was this day that changed my life forever the result of a thought that ended up being way more powerful than I ever imagined possible? I had a long plane ride to think about that, and the excitement that lay ahead. It was September 20, 1988 when I arrived at Pearson Airport, Toronto, Canada, my new home.

If I were to take a snapshot of this scene of tears and excitement and try to apply logic to it, well, it just doesn't make sense. Here's the catch: I created it. I deliberately and purposefully let the thought of emigrating take hold. When I put the idea out to the universe, I didn't realize the effect it would have.

It all started when I was working in a boring job in Waterford, Ireland. I had lots of time to let my mind wander. I remember the moment when I decided, "I want my life to be more adventurous than this. I'll live in another country." I had no idea how or when, I just had this cool idea. I imagined what it would be like. Canada was my first choice, but I wasn't going to restrict myself with limitations. I told my friend at work, and she too thought the idea was exciting, and joined in the fun. Over the next year, we talked about it every chance we had. She decided on Australia and I wanted Canada. What we didn't realize is just how powerful our thoughts could be.

Lesson #1: Time gives way to creative ideas. Ideas, nurtured properly, create reality.

I don't remember what happened next, other than I must have taken some action. I researched, talked to people, and discussed the idea with my husband and family. Family are always supportive and my husband soon entered my dream and started talking to people about it. He knew it was an exciting prospect, even though he struggled with the idea of leaving home, family, friends, and, most of all, his beloved Ireland.

Lesson #2: Determination is a fuel that moves us. Without fuel, we don't go anywhere.

The immigration process was difficult, and people delighted in telling us that it was almost impossible to get in. I didn't know it at the time, but now at 50 years of age, I realize there is something unique about me, a formula for success, that when triggered, serves me well. In my case, it is being told that I "can't" do something. Being the youngest of seven children, I learned the art of getting my way by being determined and rebellious. It is both my weakness and strength. In this case it worked in my favor. Everybody we knew who tried emigrating to Canada was turned down on the pre-application. All odds were against us.

Lesson #3: Something unique about each of us, when tapped, adds fuel to the fire.

I was in the pub one day (unusual for an Irish person I know), and a fellow I went to school with was sitting on a bar stool, elbow placed on the bar, hand poised just inches from his pint of Guinness. As I told him my thoughts, he said, "Well, fair play to ya', I've wanted to do that all my life." When I asked why he didn't, he scoffed, "Shur I'd never get in, it's freakin' impossible." I asked, "How do you know?" He responded, "Shur everybody knows that nobody's gettin' in these days. Maybe if ya win the lotto. Listen, give yer head a shake. I wish you the best of luck but we'll be talkin' 'bout it still five years from now. Shur, that's how we entertain ourselves, with them kind a thoughts."

That's what I needed to hear. I didn't think about it consciously at the time, but years later when I learned how my particular hardwiring worked, I realized that this fellow helped me be more determined than ever.

Lesson #4: Self-awareness is the key that can unlock the formula for success.

Approximately 12 months later, I was living in Canada. I came here with my husband. We knew nobody. We gave up jobs, left family and friends. I still can't explain how we managed to qualify. We landed, adapted quickly, got an apartment, and jobs. I had to pinch myself at times to be sure it wasn't all a dream.

It is now December 27, 2011. As I reflect on that day in Dublin Airport, I watch the events like a story. My husband and I still live in Canada, although we have since separated. Family still misses me, yet they know I made the right choice ... for me. I visit often because I miss them too. My friend immigrated to Australia and we stay in touch to this day. Life is strange, they say. Truth be known, it's not a bit strange, rather we're strange for taking so long to realize we make it what it is, exactly!

I was back in Ireland visiting, and I happened to be in the same pub, and low and behold, there on the same bar stool, was the same fellow. His elbow on the bar, his hand poised a few inches from his pint of Guinness. Dejà vu. If he didn't look older, I'd swear it was a time warp, or he just hadn't moved in five years. I walked up to him and told him I was home from Canada. He said, "Well, damn it, I never thought yu'da made it. I wish I had been so lucky." I looked him straight in the eye and said, "My friend, luck's got nothin' to do with it!"

Recently I learned with great excitement, that my niece, her husband, and one year old are immigrating to Canada. I live near Vancouver now and they plan to stay with me until they get settled. She visited Canada when she was a teenager, and talked about living here one day. I'm not sure she knew consciously what she was creating. They will stand at Dublin Airport on February 17, 2012 and there will be tears too, and excitement about what lies ahead. When I pick them up at Vancouver Airport, I'll be sure to tell her I remember the day she had that powerful thought, and how it led to the day they would change their lives forever.

> ***Lesson # 5: Change one belief, one thought, and you can change your life forever.***

To learn more about Christine French, visit www.expertauthorpublishing.com/cob.

Buzz Kill
Kathryn Bartman

What a day! I had a great spot on the patio. Flowers overflowed the planters, honeybees dipping lazily in and out of them. All kinds of boats were moored at the marina in front of me. Beyond the island, a few towers of craggy rock rose up above the sparkling water. The sunshine was turning tawny. The rich tapestry of this late afternoon scene was filling my senses. I started to listen past the sounds of idle conversation, gulls and boat murmurs. I was expecting the buzzing arrival of a floatplane. My husband would be on it. Almost absent-mindedly, I ignored a wasp inspecting the lime wedge I had left on the table. Once it was gone, I took a sip of my water. I smiled in anticipation of our rendezvous. Not that long ago, I would have missed this. Not that long ago, I would have waited in the parking lot with the car windows rolled all the way up. My fear of bees and wasps was a real buzz kill.

My fear of striped and stinging insects started young. I remember my sister and I climbing into the backseat of my mom's Volkswagen Bug when we were about 4 and 5. She had the bad luck to plop down on a heat-dazed bumblebee. She yelled and maybe cried a bit. The stinger caused an impressive, swollen, red bump. I was genuinely sympathetic but at the same time felt guilty. I was just <u>so grateful</u> that it wasn't <u>me</u> …

I used to both love and fear going with my family to the classic A&W fast food drive-in. The root beer looked so good in those frosted mugs, but I couldn't really enjoy it. I waited for the wasps to inevitably arrive on the tray anchored outside our partly open window. I'd be transfixed in horror as they crawled all around my now unwanted root beer. I couldn't believe it when the waitresses nonchalantly shooed them away.

If a wasp or bee got too close, I'd become frantic. The flying bullies seemed to ignore calmer people only to swoop and dive around <u>me</u>. Even our dog noticed my fear. She snapped at the air when these pests menaced me, sometimes catching and eating them.

My fear of the bicolored bugs was out of control and embarrassing.

I was stung once. My luck, it was on the nipple. At the time, the swelling from the sting about matched my breast size! As the swelling went down, however, my fear did not diminish.

As an adult, my fear of the bicolored bugs was out of control and embarrassing. When they were near, I'd twitch, contort my body to get out of the way, swat at them, or just plain freeze. Attending outdoor parties was problematic. I couldn't enjoy the festivities because I was filled with worried thoughts. Wasps were attracted to the wine and hors d'oeuvres. Wasps and bees were attracted to <u>me</u>.

The buzzing entered not just through my ears, but through my eyeballs, nostrils, and tensed lips. "Oh please," I thought, "Don't let one land on my mouth." The terrible whining pitch pinged off first one point in my skull, then another, and another. The bile of panic rose up from my guts to my throat and then into my mouth. "Go away, bee!" I screamed inside. Every muscle in my body clenched so tight that I trembled. The insect seemed to be in rhythm with my agitation.

I was in my 30's then, and I was sick and tired of these experiences.

Over the course of about six months, I found myself often thinking about my fear of bees and wasps. Slowly I began to see it more objectively. If a bee stung me, it would lose its life protecting its hive. Big consequence. For me, not much would change. I knew this because I had experience with a sting. It had been embarrassing, but not that physically painful. Part of the problem was that bees and wasps arrived unpredictably. What if I didn't let mental alarm bells go off when I saw those distinctive black and yellow stripes?

How I handle myself around cats came to mind. I don't enjoy them. Years ago, I'd learned to project an indifference to cats that stopped short of reflecting the dislike I felt inside. Before I learned this, cats would single me out in a room for special attention. Now they don't. Funnily enough, I've come to think cats aren't half bad.

If I similarly clamped down on my fear response and "ignored" bees and wasps, was it possible they would ignore me too? People who weren't afraid of bees just seemed to ignore them. In general, they were also not pestered by them. I had some thoughts that were brand new for me: What if I pretended I was relaxed around bees and wasps? What if I pretended I didn't care if they were around or not? Then: I am willing to try this. I want to try this. I can do this.

And I did!

I learned that I could control my body's reaction to those bees and wasps. When I didn't freak out, they ignored me. I faked it for a while, but what started as an act became my new reality. Over the past few years, I occasionally have had to remind myself to cool it and not react by sending out that fear vibe, but it always works.

Recently, I was at the trailhead of a recommended hike in a gorgeous national park. The Park Rangers had posted a handwritten sign: "Warning—Aggressive bees reported along this trail. Use caution!" I smiled and took a picture of the sign. Then I started the hike, keeping my camera out. There were going to be lots of scenic spots along the way.

To learn more about Kathryn Bartman, visit www.expertauthorpublishing.com/cob.

Taking Inspired Action and Investing in Myself
Lisa Sasevich

I was sitting there staring at my computer, having been recently let go from a company that taught women how to understand men. Male spouses, bosses and sons operate differently from females, and once women understood this, I saw their relationships and their lives transform before my eyes. It was work I loved, and I believed it would be my life's work. It was difficult to see anything good coming from this ending, but the work I devoted myself to there had taught me how to fill workshops by crafting irresistible offers and closing sales without being salesy.

I was using that experience now, coaching people one-on-one to help them grow their businesses. I took the last company I worked for from $300,000 to $1.3 million annually in three years.

There it was again. The email that just wouldn't go away, offering a workshop on how to take your business online. I wanted to expand beyond one client at a time and reach more people, but the workshop cost $3,000. My husband and I didn't have that kind of money in our sock drawers.

I'd been ignoring this recurring email for weeks, but I couldn't stare at it any longer. I clicked on it. They had added an offer for a six-payment option. It was March, and the workshop wasn't until November. Even with six payments, that was still $500 a month—more than a car payment.

I turned it over again in my mind, and at that point *I just couldn't not do it.* I had taken my business as far as it could go—to $130,000 a year—by listening to experts' free calls and teleclasses, trading advice with people, paying attention to different marketing campaigns and reading books. But I had plateaued. I could not take on one more client. I had no time. I had little kids (ages 1 and 3). And I was the breadwinner.

I'd been stuck at six figures for many years. No matter the job, I would get to about six figures and just stay there. Of course that was a huge accomplishment, but I just knew I had more in me.

So I did it. I did the six pay. I paid the three grand and I got myself to the workshop in November.

But it was what happened in the intervening months that really changed my belief...

Just from making that investment, I felt different. This was the first time I invested a big chunk of money into my "blessing," my expertise, my own business. In the six months before I even got to the workshop, I started selling VIP days for $3,000. I sold eight of them very quickly.

My mind would never have thought of that had I not taken the action to invest at that level myself. I had opened the door for people to *invest in me* at that level.

Shortly after, I took some of the money I made and invested it in another course. This was a 10-week,

$7,500 course. Within three weeks of starting that course, I started selling a $7,500 program.

I began to understand the relationship of making the investment in myself and then really having courage and the mojo to be able to sell my own programs at that level. By making the investment, I knew it was possible and easy for someone to see that they needed what I had to offer, and to dig deep to pay for it, because I had done that.

It started me thinking in new ways. It gave me ideas, and I began to pay attention to things that I just couldn't see before I took that risk. I saw that I could package my services in a different way that I never thought of before, charging a much higher rate, and serving people at a higher level because of this structure. I was finally giving myself a raise.

At last, I made it to the November workshop—the biggest event of all. At the end, they made an offer for a year-long mentorship program with a $20,000 level and a $100,000 level. I knew the offer was coming, and I never thought I'd have any interest. But the $3,000 investment earned me $24,000. And the $7,500 investment brought in $30,000.

All I could think was: What would happen if I made a $100,000 investment in myself? I couldn't even imagine it.

Sitting there, I felt expansion in my chest at the prospect of joining the mastermind. One part of me is rising up, wanting to scream, "Yes!" And then there's a part coming down from my head, saying, "You can't, it's inconvenient, you don't have the money..." Big Me is arguing with Little Me—My Heart, my Higher Self, my knowing, and Source are arguing with My Head, the scared part, the part that wants to stay comfortable and small.

It turned out to be a very good indicator that it was time to go for it.

I learned that it's never convenient and it's always scary—that's how you know it's the right thing.

"If you're looking for a quantum leap in your business and expecting it to be convenient and comfortable, you're using the wrong indicators."

Here I was turning 40. And my husband was in the last year of his cardiothoracic surgery fellowship. After 10 long years, he would be a heart surgeon, he'd be making money. Life was about to get very comfortable. If I didn't do this now, I'd miss my window. It was my last chance to have enough hunger and enough fire to find out what I could achieve.

Seven months after I signed up, I started enrolling clients in $100,000 coaching programs, and I still am. I'm probably the market leader in that today.

Entrepreneurs who are 30-year veterans are learning how to do it from me—mentors I only dreamed of meeting three years ago are now my students. And the number one thing I say is, "You need to be the client you want to attract."

If you want clients to invest, invest in yourself.

If you want people refunding from your programs, ask for a refund. If you want people saying, "I'll think about it," go think about it. If you want decisive clients, be decisive. If you want clients to invest, invest in yourself.

My business is helping Animal Communicators make $200,000 a year; Belief Change Experts are breaking six figures; all kinds of holistic practitioners are selling $5,000 and $10,000 and $20,000 programs. And the part I love the most is they're making big money doing what they love and what they were designed to do.

I didn't know I was going to have a $2 million year. I joined the $100,000 mastermind and I went from $130,000 to $2.2 million that year. The next year I made $4.4 million. And we're on track to do it again. And again.

That's a huge leap and it represents an overwhelming number of people I was able to help with my gifts. I couldn't have uttered that I wanted to make a million dollars and change the lives of thousands of messengers. I just wanted to learn a lot and at least make my $100,000 back.

There are times when one door closes and you have no idea what's ahead. And you get a glimmer of something, but you don't even know the whole story of what it is and why it's calling you forward. But you need to honor that piece of you that's rising up inside. And the way you know it's rising up is there's another piece of you pushing it down. It's not always clear, it's not always comfortable, and it's *never* convenient. But what is it worth to know you've lived up to your potential? ***How can you not?***

> *To learn more about Lisa Sasevich, visit*
> *www.expertauthorpublishing.com/cob.*

The Perfect Job
Bonnie Hope McDonald

Many times in conversations with people, I hear, "There are no good jobs" or "It's so hard to find a job." What if the job they already have is the perfect job? Or what if the perfect job is waiting for everyone right now?

What if our path needs to wind a bit around the bend before we reach our destination? Here is a look at a few well-known people and the jobs they had before their big successes:

- Dishwasher at a Chinese Restaurant—Michael Dell the founder and CEO of Dell
- Ambulance Driver—Walt Disney
- Janitor—Jim Carrey
- Pool Boy, Gas Station Attendant and Firefighter—Clint Eastwood
- Dressing as a Giant Chicken for a Mexican Restaurant—Brad Pitt
- Soda Shop Girl—Lucille Ball

It took me many years to realize that every job I have ever had was the perfect job at that time of my life. No other job would have been better.

Let me explain. My first job at 12 years old was cleaning horse corrals for a neighbor. I was paid $1.00 an hour. Unfortunately the stalls hadn't been cleaned out in a long time, so many weeks of hard labor went by before I saw bare earth. It was stinky work, with horseflies buzzing around and tiny black gnats in my hair and eyes. Not exactly pleasant, but it was the perfect job. I was able to ride horses for free, and buy clothes and school supplies—and that made me happy.

During my college days I volunteered at a veterinarian's office, as I had always dreamed of being a vet since age 10. It was challenging to help with cleaning the cages, holding animals in appointments, and even assisting with surgeries. Ultimately, the job was too sad for me. I thought I would be helping pets get well. The reality was that many pets were at the end of their lives or the pet owners were unable to afford the medical fees. But it was the perfect job at the time because I saw that it was okay for me to try a job to see if it fit. I learned that if it doesn't, we can move on and know that our dreams may not always become reality. If I hadn't worked there, there's a part of me that would still be wondering whether I could have been a vet. By taking that job, I now know the answer.

In my 20's I worked for the U.S. Postal Service. I was living in a rural area in the Mojave Desert. My first day on the job I walked more than six hours in over 100° F heat. I ended up with blisters the size of quarters on the bottom of my feet. Hobbling for weeks and sweating in the heat, I realized what it is to work hard for the money. But it was the perfect job. It taught me that we trade precious hours and minutes of our lives for money ... and that I needed more than just a paycheck to make the trade worthwhile.

For 13 years I wrote a weekly food column in a small town in the Mojave Desert. My salary was a free 50-cent newspaper. That wasn't much pay, but it was the perfect job because the payoff was huge. I was paid over and over again with opportunities that came my way.

Writing the food column brought me much joy and happiness. I looked forward to researching the recipe of the week, alternating between breakfast, lunch, dinner and dessert. Often readers requested a certain recipe. This was pre-internet so I would peruse my collection of over 200 cookbooks or head to the library where they had over 1000 cookbooks.

When construction began on a new grocery store, I knew that I wanted to apply. Jobs were few and far between in the Mojave Desert and I wanted to work for this new store. During the interview I gave my qualifications: working in a fried chicken fast food establishment, cashier at a health food store, tractor driver, Girl Friday ... and writing a weekly food column for the local newspaper. The interviewer's eyes became larger and brighter, he leaned forward in his seat and then he said, "Really? You write a food column?" I was hired as the Deli Manager for the store right out of the starting gate. Two other opportunities from that column were overseeing the first Natural New Products contest at the largest Natural Products convention on the West Coast, and becoming a judge at a food contest in California City, California.

Loving what we do energizes us.

In my 30s I moved into the natural foods industry where I flourished for many years and enjoyed what I considered to be the perfect job. Within the industry I worked in retail, wholesale, and as a manufacturing representative. All were perfect jobs. I learned that loving what we do energizes us and makes our heart sing.

Now that I am in my 50s, I have recreated myself. I am an entrepreneur and writer, sharing my life lessons, encouraging others to know that life is full of choices, that we have unlimited opportunities, and that when we love what we do, and yet count our blessings for what we have right now, life rewards us with boundless joy, happiness and energy—and our hearts will sing.

Take a few minutes right now to reflect on your jobs, your work, your life, and count your blessings. You will then know that every job you have had in your life has been the perfect job; that you are holding your life in your own hands; that "The Perfect Job" is not "out there," but that you have the perfect job right now.

To learn more about Bonnie Hope McDonald, visit www.expertauthorpublishing.com/cob.

The Big Guy with a Pink Feather Boa
Jen Cochran

I walked up the cement stairs with my two teenage sons in tow and knocked on the door of my ex-husband's home. It was Father's Day, and his turn to have the kids. My boys opened the door and entered hesitantly. Something wasn't right. My ex met us in the entryway. He picked up his phone and made a call. I heard him yell at the person on the other end of the line, "I'm going to shoot an intruder!" Then he started walking to the place he kept his gun. We all froze in fear. "GET OUT!" I yelled to my sons as he moved toward the gun. "RUN!" My precious boys stood unblinking. Their father was moving quickly, nervous sweat running in rivers down his face. I saw his hands tremble awkwardly as he pulled the nine-millimeter gun out of the kitchen drawer. I knew this was it. He had finally gone over the edge. As the gun settled into his hands, he pointed it at me. His arms were shaking, he couldn't hold it still. He pushed the safety off and I heard the loud metal click of a gun being cocked. I knew I was dead if I didn't run, and that's what I did, I turned and ran. I ran out the front door of his house and I didn't stop running until I got to the end of the street. Tears streamed down my face as I called 911 and told them what happened.

We had been divorced for 10 years, and he was remarried. It was supposed to be a special day for fathers and their kids. I thought this kind of incident was in the past!

I fell into a dark depression. Every day I woke up I was certain it was my last. I felt like an abused animal with a choke chain around my neck. Every move I made, I made with him in mind. Fear dictated my every step. I felt paralyzed, trapped, violated and unsafe—utterly helpless and hopeless.

I hated him. I wished he were dead. My mind was consumed with storm clouds of rage. I had panic attacks when he was near me at our court dates; I felt as if my heart would beat out of my chest and I could hardly keep my legs steady beneath me. I could not be in the same room with him and maintain any semblance of sanity. My fractured foundation was crumbling and my world was falling apart. I was diagnosed with Post Traumatic Stress Disorder and my physical health was faltering. Any strength I had left was fading fast. Something had to give.

I had been fighting with this man for 15 years. My mother told me God was trying to teach me something—and for once in my life I heard her words. What could my soul learn? What action was I supposed to take? Over the course of time I tried everything: forgiving him, praying for him, fighting him, forgiving him again. It felt like carousel monsters on a painful merry-go-round ride that never stopped.

The day came when I could take no more. I stopped, surrendered and fell to my knees. Like a hurricane, my anguish could not be contained. Defeated, my head bowed and my shoulders dropped. Every ugly, painful emotion I had been avoiding and denying for over a decade bubbled up from the depths of my being, through me and out of me. I wailed in grief, my insides twisted in nausea and hurt. I felt as if I was going to die. I had no strength left to fight the raging storm. I was swept along like a ragdoll, fear and anxiety consumed me—body, mind and soul. I allowed the emotions to have their way with me. I was done running, I was done hiding. I embraced and accepted my fear and I felt it down to my bones. Then something unexpected and miraculous happened—the storm was beginning to subside. The clouds began to lift, gently dissolving and melting into a cloudless cornflower-blue sky.

> *I say what I feel, and it is not a reflection of anyone else around me.*

In that moment I realized no one has control over my emotions or the way I feel. I acknowledged my feelings and thanked them for doing their best to keep me safe. I was beginning to understand my feelings are MY feelings. I have to own them and I have to feel them. Now I don't have to run, hide or escape. I just have to own, allow and tell my truth. I say what I feel, and it is not a reflection of anyone else around me. Another revelation occurred: I had been more afraid of my own feelings than of this man.

I love the saying: "A nervous breakdown can be the beginning of a nervous breakthrough," and that was the case for me. The feelings I had resisted for so long were my doorway to freedom.

The funny thing was as soon as I had my breakdown/breakthrough, my ex—and everyone else in my life—started treating me very differently. I believe this is because I am finally doing something different. I respect myself. After realizing I no longer needed to be afraid, I considered what would make me happy. The image that brought me the greatest joy was my ex wearing a belly shirt, tights, and a pink feather boa . . . shaking a tambourine. Now if anxiety begins to threaten, I consider this visual and instantly experience relief and laughter.

I am grateful for the storm that took me over that day and I have profound appreciation for the emotions that brought me to my knees. One of the greatest revelations I have ever had is that painful emotions aren't bad. <u>All</u> feelings have their place on the canvas of human experience and I respect them: The anxiety, fear and grief as well as the joy, laughter and love. I believe because I was willing to descend to the depths I can now reach the heights of emotion and enjoy everything this human adventure has to offer.

Now my intention is to support other women who have experienced abuse and help them find their center, feel their feelings, use their voice and claim their authentic power. This is my purpose, my passion and my life—and it has *never* been better!

To learn more about Jen Cochran, visit www.expertauthorpublishing.com/cob.

Faith
Nicole Daga

I can't say I've ever fully embraced the idea of religion or God. I've always felt the whole thing read like a bad movie script with too many holes in the plot. There were too many questions unanswered and I always wanted to challenge religious figures in their beliefs in search of some sort of revelation. It's not that I didn't believe, it's that my doubts and logical side steered me away from committing to that belief.

In January 2010 my world was shaken. My mother called me and broke the news to me that she had been diagnosed with breast cancer. My mother has and always will be everything to me. We are a part of each other that cannot be defined by conventional terms. She is my soul mate, my best friend, and the very best part of who I am. To say the news of this was daunting is an understatement of drastic proportions. We were confident though, all the doctors were optimistic, and my mother and I were determined that we could beat it. We could face anything if we did it together because our love was stronger than anything we could come up against. She told me she had everything to live for and she was going to fight, and so she did. She began to fight and I began to pray.

Every once in awhile I would come to my knees and bow my head at the edge of my bed and pray that the ones I loved would be happy and healthy. I never asked for material things, all I wanted was for those I loved the most in the world to live full and happy lives. I wanted them to laugh, to love, and to remember every second along the way. Now I prayed every night that my mother would see her way through this and that God would grant us time. I needed to believe that our time together had only just begun and that we would have time to play with the grandkids I had yet to give her, go to Disneyland as she always wanted to, and live next door to each other so that every day could be a mother / daughter day. I prayed for time, I prayed for health, I prayed for happiness, and I never allowed myself to believe that those prayers fell on deaf ears.

My mother went through two surgeries, seven out of eight rounds of aggressive chemotherapy and a month of radiation treatments five days a week. There were times when she wanted to quit, when it was just too hard, but she stayed strong. Even though she never said it, I know that she did it for me. She wanted to be here as much as I needed her to be. She was my hero and an inspiration to me every day to be stronger and braver. We spent Christmas together with a renewed gratitude for what we had. My mother and I never took each other for granted. I told her every day how much I loved her, how she is the heart that beats inside of me, the voice that guides me, and the spirit that carries me. We hugged and kissed each other and truly believed that our prayers had been answered. She was feeling great, the doctors were happy with her progress. My mother was on her way to recovery and the beautiful Mediterranean trip that she and my father were finally going to take.

In February 2011 my mom came to visit me in Vancouver, where she started to get a bad cough. When she returned home, she saw her doctor and was diagnosed and given antibiotics. The medication wasn't working. After several trips to the doctor and specialist, misdiagnoses and various medications, the cough only got worse. She was checked into the hospital in March after x-rays and a biopsy with a diagnosis of breast cancer. It had managed to spread to her lungs despite our best efforts. On April 26, 2011 I lost my mom. She passed away peacefully in her sleep at the hospice with my dad and me by her side.

I wanted to be angry with God more than I wanted my mom back. How could he take her from me when he knew how much I loved her, how much I needed her? I felt a hollowness within myself that could never be filled. Then in one moment things changed: I recognized that maybe my mother wasn't taken from me as a punishment but as a mercy. God didn't want to see her suffer anymore. I recognized and accepted a different version of the story. I do not believe that God controls everything that happens in our lives like a puppet master pulling strings. But I do believe he is there to give us strength to help us through.

Having faith will keep you safe and warm in the midst of life's storms.

I'm not about to stand on a podium and preach to others about a higher power, but I will say this—given the choice of believing in a higher power or not believing at all, I now choose to believe. Having faith will keep you safe and warm in the midst of life's storms. It will give you strength and comfort when you need it most. Faith by definition is belief that is not based on proof. It is a choice that you make every day based on nothing but a blind trust. You have nothing to lose by believing. I honestly believe that my mother is with me every day and she is in a place where peace and contentment is breathed in and out like air. She will forever be in my heart, and when I come to my knees and bow my head, I speak to her. And I know she is listening—not because I can hear her, but because I trust it in my heart.

To learn more about Nicole Daga, visit www.expertauthorpublishing.com/cob.

Comedy of Terrors
Robert Calvert

*"To be, or not to be —
is that the question?
Whether tis nobler
in the mind I suffered"*

There is a dream most stage actors have experienced at one time or another, and it consists of being on stage and not knowing your lines. I know this, because in my 30-year acting career I have starred in this dream many times.

Not so long ago, I was cast in a farce at one of the local dinner theatres. Due to a mysterious run of ailments and injuries, we had to shuffle cast roles several times. Because of my knee injury, I ended up eventually replacing the director. My starting task as director was to replace the star actor, which evidently was—Myself. No easy task (just kidding).

One Saturday morning during the show's run I received a call from the owner of the dinner theatre. Apparently one of the main actors had become very ill following the previous night's performance and was in the hospital. Could I come to the theatre at 4:00 p.m. that afternoon and learn his lines? I don't really know why I agreed to such an insane request, however—"THE SHOW MUST GO ON."

At this point I began to feel the dream slowly becoming reality.

After two hours rehearsing and going over exits and entrances, I realized there was no way I was going to pull this off. Our stage manager's solution was "mic him." I loved the idea—the booth could feed my lines to me while I was on stage.

*(The lights dim ... The curtain rises ...
I step out onto the stage)*

I was unconcerned as the curtain went up and I was pushed out onto the stage with several other actors. The fun began when the techie in the booth was calling cues to the stage manager backstage, as well as feeding me my lines. Now, what line was for me, and what was banter between the stage manager and the booth?

(I clear my throat ... and take a breath...)

At the exact moment it was to be said, my line would come to me through my earpiece—which created a delay in my delivery. When I finally received it, I didn't know to whom I was supposed to deliver it. (This brought a whole new meaning to the word farce.)

The cast couldn't keep a straight face while they waited for me to say my lines and deliver them to the wrong actors. They looked like they were like watching a newscast from the other side of the world. In the confusion, I didn't know when to leave or which door to exit. Once pushed off stage, I was immediately grabbed by the costume people, stripped down to my underwear, fitted with a new costume, mic, and earpiece, and thrust back on stage.

Now sporting a "superman" costume I "leaped in a single bound" back onto the stage; and, realizing I didn't know what I was supposed to do, resorted to the classic superman pose, with my hands on my hips and my legs slightly apart. I looked over at one of the lead actors on stage and saw that he had cracked up laughing. I was eventually escorted to a window I was to fly out of as my exit—like a bird, or a plane ... or something. We had a mattress on the floor for superman's grand leap. The problem was my injured knee. There was no way I could have jumped out that window, even landing on a mattress. So I just stood on the ledge and kind of ... stepped onto the mattress and walked away ... the audience roared. I realized how silly this must have looked from an audience perspective. However sometimes it's best not to worry about what others think, put a smile on your face and keep going.

Halfway into act two and I was once again being escorted off stage by a grinning co-actor for another unknown costume change. However, the wire to my mic and earpiece snapped in half. Panic set in.

(To be, or not ... to be me ...)

I was only half-dressed and my entrance was fast approaching. The stage manager scrambled to find me another body mic. As my confidence wavered, the stage manager ran back to me and whispered, "I found one, and you are now late for your entrance." Fitted with the new mic and earpiece and the rest of my costume, I was thrust back on, landing right down center stage. The audience roared, and the cast joined in the folly.

Dazed from the panic backstage, I really had no idea why they were all laughing. I was unaware I was wearing a long blond wig and a beard that wasn't on quite right. It was tucked under my exposed chin. I had on a long jacket that looked like a dress, and the mic and earpiece the stage manager had found to replace the broken one wasn't the right kind. I hadn't realized, but it had a mouthpiece on it that came down across my cheek to my mouth. So I looked like Britney Spears on testosterone.

The new mic and earpiece body pack now made it imperative that it be tested with the stage manager on every costume change. Getting tired of my incessant requests, she told me, on my last entrance of the night, "It's working, don't worry about it." So it didn't get tested. Well, I got on stage and guess what? It didn't work.

The dream had finally come true.

> ***Don't let fear stop you from
> trying something different.***

The cast was laughing hysterically as I would lean out the doors and the windows for someone backstage to feed me a line or two to keep me going. In the end, I realized fear was just an illusion, a limiting concept of the mind; so don't let fear stop you from stepping out of your comfort zone and trying something different.

If we continue to sleepwalk through life in the safety of our scripted lives, we may never experience the joy of breaking free of our fears and following the dreams of our hearts.

The dread of being on stage without lines ... or finding oneself in life without direction ... was much scarier than the actual reality.

And the adventure of spirit prevailed.

(I bow ... the curtain comes down ... applause!)

To learn more about Robert Calvert, visit www.expertauthorpublishing.com/cob.

Forgiveness Brings Freedom
Barbara Halcrow, MSW

He brought out his handkerchief and started to cry. This wasn't the first time I'd seen him cry or tell his war stories, but somehow this was different, maybe because I was different. "You know Barb, those were good men," he said, wiping his tears away. He'd had a couple of beers by now. Though his mind was sharp, he was a man of few words when it came to his feelings, except when he drank.

Before marrying my mother, Gordon had been an RCAF bombadier in WWII. He and his men did practice runs off Boundary Bay, BC. One night a bomb malfunctioned and exploded, sending their Liberator Bomber into the Pacific Ocean more than three miles from the nearest shoreline.

As a young lawyer, Gordon was known for his cleverness and brilliance. He was handsome, well liked and humorous. He also loved nature. He knew every river, lake and mountain throughout British Columbia. His sister said he should've been a Fish and Game Warden; it would have been less stressful. I'm not so sure—he loved the courtroom challenge.

He was known for other things too, like abandoning his wife and four children and letting his law practice dissolve into alcoholism. At times his recklessness and appearance as a drunken derelict belied his true stature.

Today though, he looked good in suit and tie. He was now in a veteran's retirement center where his drinking was more controlled. Dad seemed happier, although he still limped badly from a hip fracture. I felt cautiously pleased to see him.

"What happened next, Dad?" I ventured, as he wiped his eyes again. I already knew what happened next, I'd heard him talk about this incident many times. This time, though, I felt more open. I knew it was important for Dad to retell the experience that haunted his life.

"Just a minute—I'll have one more," he said to the waiter. Dad was allowed controlled outings to a nearby bar. "Well, Barb it was a helluva time. Pitch black, couldn't see a bloody thing. The plane disappeared. My men were yelling. We swam hard, but that water was damn icy." He paused. "You know, they never made it," he said quietly. "I'm sorry," I murmured. He choked back a few more tears. The waiter came over.

"You all right, Gordon?"

"Yeh, Jim, just talking to my daughter, here." He shored himself up.

"I could hear them," he carried on stoically, "They were calling for help, but I had to keep swimming, it was too cold. You know," he looked past me, "I could see some distant lights on the shore, but I couldn't go any further. I felt like I was going to die. I prayed to the Lord and said goodbye to my dad, mom, and all my brothers and sisters. Then the strangest thing happened. My foot touched a sandbar. I couldn't believe it. Barb, it was a miracle. It really was. I wanted to be a minister after that. I felt it was my calling." He took a sip of beer, his eyes still misty.

For me it had been a long journey—always missing my father, never knowing how or where he was. He'd been gone for most of my life since I was nine years old except for sporadic visits in my teens during his attempts at sobriety. Over the years I tried to bury my feelings about my father, thinking he didn't care about me, my siblings or my mother. Inside I'd never forgiven him for leaving us. My thoughts of him always brought me pain, sadness and shame.

Once, traveling with my high school girls' basketball team, our bus stopped at a small terminal. Suddenly an inebriated, disheveled man entered, swearing loudly and demanding service. We stared at him in annoyance. One of my teammates, Linda, was a neighbor and knew my dad. She glanced at me. "Barbara, isn't that your father?"

Feelings of shame and hurt overwhelmed me. I put my head down in humiliation. I'd seen Dad like this too often. I shook my head and quietly said, "No, that's not my father." It wasn't my nature to be dishonest. I felt like I was betraying my father *and* myself. I wanted to run out of the terminal, but he was quickly escorted outside.

Today, as I sat in the local pub with Dad, I saw his pain and sadness and the burden he still carried as the sole survivor of that tragic plane crash. My compassion deepened. It was clear he never fully recovered from his war trauma.

His recent move to the veteran's retirement home allowed him to heal his wounds, among other war veterans who understood trauma and loss. He'd been given a chance to regain a sense of life purpose.

"You know, Barb," Dad suddenly said, looking directly at me with his hazel eyes, "I'm proud of you." "You've done well in your life. I've really missed you kids." He looked away.

I felt his words, his sincerity. I'd not heard many words of acknowledgment from my father since childhood. "Thank you, Dad," I said softly.

I was surprised that he missed us. I never knew he felt that way until that very moment; that his separation from us had been as painful for him as it was for all of us. I sat back and felt my tears well up.

As we returned to the retirement center, I told him I'd visit him again. When I drove away, he did not go directly inside. He just stood there leaning on his cane, watching me leave. I felt tearful again as my heart filled with warmth and compassion. Although he was still my father, I saw him as a man who had gone through some painful, life-altering experiences; a man who just wanted to share his heart with me and convey to me, that yes, he did care.

I knew that holding onto my hurt and anger kept my own pain alive. With my heart open, I wanted to fully let go of all the pain and resentment. I'd made other attempts at forgiving my father, but this time seeing him still so wounded and vulnerable brought me a depth of compassion and understanding I'd never had before.

In that moment of letting go came a quiet opening within me.

I forgave my father that day, and in that moment of letting go came a quiet opening within me. Years of hurt and resentful feelings were surrendered and melted away. I felt released. My belief about forgiveness forever changed that day. Forgiveness brings not only peace of mind, it opens the doors of the heart to freedom.

To learn more about Barbara Halcrow, visit www.expertauthorpublishing.com/cob.

A Transformational Turning Point
Eva Gregory, CPCC

The Law of Attraction not only saved my life, but it became my life. I thought I knew all the answers, and was on the fast track to a successful and prosperous life. Boy was I wrong. My life partner, Robin, and I ran a software company in California and it was leaking money like the proverbial sieve. For over five years, we had been searching for backing to help us launch the fantastic software program that we had patented—but to no avail. We were laying off staff, not paying ourselves in order to retain the crew we had and morale was not just low, but non-existent. We had creditors after us personally, as well as after the business and the stress level was incredibly high.

During what seemed to be our darkest hour, I had a major aha moment. I had been studying metaphysics for years, as I found it extremely compelling, but I only understood it intellectually. I really did not understand how to apply it to my life until I stumbled upon a universal principle called the Law of Attraction. It was as though the light bulb came on, the fireworks went off, and I finally really got it!

Basically, the Law of Attraction says whatever you are focused on you will get more of—whether wanted or not. But what I realized is that it is the *emotion*—the emotional charge you have on whatever you're focused on, that is magnetizing to you more of the same. This was the missing component from my life.

Imagine where my focus had set up residence. "We don't have enough funds." We can't make the payroll." "We will lose the business." I'd been focusing on exactly what I did *not* want more of in my life! The thoughts I was repeating to myself, that focus on the lack of what I wanted was the engine, but the highly charged negative emotion I was carrying was the fuel that was magnetizing even more of what I did not want into my existence. Moreover, I had taken it to the ultimate level, as everyone within the company was simply amping up that vibration to gargantuan proportions.

Once I grasped the principle, I felt I had nothing to lose by introducing the concept to the rest of the company. In order to change the vibe of the company by shifting our emotions, as a team we created a company-wide game with a huge spreadsheet called the *Prosperity Account*, based on *The Prosperity Game,* a process I had learned about through Abraham-Hicks.

The game went like this. On Day 1, $10,000 was deposited into the account and everyone in the company was asked to post to the spreadsheet how the funds would be spent. Each day the account was increased by an additional $1,000. So $11,000 was deposited on Day Two, $12,000 on Day Three, etc. After a bit, I was surprised to see how generous people were being. Since there was no fear of the funds dwindling, department members were making purchases for other departments besides their own. The money in our imaginary *Prosperity Account* was flowing and we were actually having some *fun*, for the first time in a long while. The goal of the game was to get our focus on something that felt better than where it had been for a very long time. The experiment worked. Overall, the company energy shifted and many of us began to look forward to coming to work again. The success of the Law of Attraction actively working through the *Prosperity Account* was only the beginning for me.

The Universe only notices the essence of where we are focusing our energy and thoughts, and assumes it is real.

What I have come to know is that the Universe does not know if what we are focused on is real or imaginary. It only notices the essence of where we are focusing our energy and thoughts, and assumes it is real. Therefore, as far as the Universe was concerned, prosperity *was* our reality. The *Prosperity Account* exercise showed me that no matter what I spent my money in the account on that day, there would always be more in the account tomorrow. So, I was able to stop thinking of lack and living in lack, as there was always an abundance of monetary flow. The exercise taught me to stretch my wealth mentality, a valuable lesson that must be learned in order to allow prosperity to follow.

And follow it, I did. Within nine months of launching the *Prosperity Account* exercise, we were approached to sell the company, lock, stock, and barrel. We went from living from *no paycheck* to *no paycheck* (as Robin and I were not always collecting one for ourselves), to successfully selling the business for a hefty sum of money.

Why? Because we were in a good place mentally and were able to see the opportunity for what it was and act on it!

Learning about the Law of Attraction and actually experiencing how it works was the most transformational turning point in my life. I learned that the difference between feeling hopeful and feeling fearful is the difference between success and failure. Fearfulness was not a good feeling, so through the *Prosperity Account*, I found a way to grab onto thoughts that made me feel better which made the key monumental shift. If one has to choose between feeling bad and feeling good, what is the logical choice? Seems simple. Simple—not necessarily easy—depending on your belief systems and where you have been focused over time. Yet, it *can* be that simple—I just had to let go of my old way of doing things and embrace a new way.

To learn more about Eva Gregory, visit www.expertauthorpublishing.com/cob.

Rif-sen, My Four-Legged Soul Mate
Romana Van Lissum

The number 13 has always been considered a "bad luck" number for a lot of people. For me, it's the complete opposite. My dream came true (almost 31 years ago!) on April 23, 1981, on my 13th birthday. I still remember it like it was yesterday.

Growing up, I drove my parents insane as I continuously pleaded, cried and begged them to buy me a horse. On my 13th birthday, my wish came true and I was presented with a beautiful chestnut-colored mare. It was love at first sight. She eyed me with curiosity and sniffed my hand, but all I could do was just stand there and take in her beauty. She was tall with white socks on her right front and hind legs, and she had a unique blaze that ran down the front of her face in the shape of a question mark with the dot ending between her nostrils. She was a registered half Arabian, and her name was Rif-sen. Also, I was told that our birthdays were very close together, separated by just six days.

I instantly fell in love and couldn't believe that she was all mine! Visions of us running through fields and going on grand adventures together were all I could think about. I knew I would confess all my girly secrets, hopes and desires to her. She would be my confidante and teacher while I would be her protector and best friend. I was making detailed plans as I stroked her soft fur, lost in my thoughts.

Over the years, Rify and I bonded in a special and magical way. I felt it and others around us saw it too. I knew we had something special and I think she felt it as well. She was truly my soul mate, she just happened to be a horse.

She followed me into strange horse trailers, over rough paths and through deep streams. I took her swimming in ponds and entered her in local horse shows. She went everywhere and anywhere I asked her to. Any horseperson knows that a horse is a fight-or-flight animal, and can be unreliable or even dangerous in a scary or unfamiliar situation. That is why thousands of people are hurt every year around horses, and why it was so amazing that Rify trusted me the way she did.

Rify and I trusted each other completely. As a young, crazy teenager, my wild ideas were constantly landing us in unusual or even dangerous predicaments. During these times, I was never, ever hurt. I can only imagine her thoughts, "Ok, I'll do this if you want, but only against my better judgment—and only because it's you! By the way, your mom would freak out if she knew we were doing this!" She was such a good sport.

When I got older, life started to get in the way of my horses. I eventually moved out with a boyfriend and later married and had a daughter. My focus shifted to working and making money and some traveling, but I never forgot about Rify. When my husband and I got the chance to move to 2½ acres, we took it. We moved Rify and her daughter My Reason to our property so I could finally take full responsibility for them.

The last few years of Rify's life, she suffered from an injury that worsened as she aged. I made her as comfortable as possible with pain medication. It was a very stressful time and I constantly worried about how much pain she was in. After many tests and x-rays, my vet gave me the earth-shattering news. It was time to let her go. I made the dreaded appointment.

The night before, I stayed in her stall with her. I snuggled with her and told her how much I loved her as I buried my face in her mane and sobbed. It scared me to think of life without my girl. I felt frantic and out of control as I inhaled her scent for the last time. I buried my face in her neck and promised her I would never forget.

The next day was sunny and the vet was scheduled to arrive in the afternoon. I let both horses into the backyard to graze for a few hours as I sat on the edge of the deck in silence watching them. I fed them a full bag of carrots while brushing and stroking Rify. I didn't want to let her go, but I had to think of her. It's the hardest decision I've had to make, and I fight with my feelings of guilt and sorrow even now.

The vet arrived. My emotions took hold of me as I lost control and sobbed, stroking her and telling her how much I loved her. I kissed her eyes and ran my hands over her ears and down her face. Between sobs, I kept whispering, "Good girl Rify, I love you. Good girl Rify, I love you." The procedure was quick and painless.

"She's gone. There's no spark in her eye." I said out loud in a small, dull voice. I pulled the small pair of scissors out of my back pocket and cut away a big chunk of her mane. Then I pulled the elastic out of my hair and tied the horsehair together in a nice neat pile. Later, I got a heart-shaped locket so I could keep a small tuft of her mane with me always. It was therapeutic and comforting to have her near me like that.

Growing up, I was a very impatient teenager who felt insecure in my body and very lost most of the time. Rify came at just the right time. I loved animals but I didn't realize that loving an animal meant more than just having empathy for them. It meant that there are no days off from mucking out a stall or dragging pails of water from the house in -30° winter temperatures, just because it's cold outside or I didn't feel like it. It also meant putting my birthday money aside to buy her a winter blanket instead of buying some new clothes for myself. Rify was an important part of my life. She taught me responsibility, routine, confidence, structure, patience and compassion. She was a wonderful, patient teacher who carried me for miles in the hot sun while I bounced along unbalanced on her spine, learning to ride bareback. We had a strong bond and connection that very few people are lucky to experience with their pet.

Over time, the smiles outweigh the tears.

For now, I still have a piece of her; her beautiful daughter who will turn 28 years old in 10 days. Rify's photo sits on my night table and it's rare that a day goes by that I don't think about her. The pain never goes away, but then one day you wake up, and instead of breaking down in tears, you smile. Over time, the smiles outweigh the tears. You just learn to live with the grief and focus more on the happy memories.

Losing a loved one or pet is never easy. One thing I know is that the memories are important and they keep your soul alive. Instead of concentrating on the painful days, I choose to remember the good times, especially the best day of all—the day that an inexperienced and insecure 13-year old girl and a young 4-year old horse fell in love and became soul mates.

To learn more about Romana Van Lissum, visit www.expertauthorpublishing.com/cob.

The Other Mother
Michele de Reus

Ian and I had been divorced for less than a year and the days we traded our four-year old son, Cole, were uncomfortable and awkward. For a few hours after being dropped off, Cole liked to spend one-on-one time with me. We did a variety of activities during these hours and this day we were playing Candyland, a popular board game. Cole looked up at me, and with a glimmer in his eyes he proudly said, "Dad and Lisa are getting married." "Oh?," I stammered, "Thaaat's cool." I found my heart beating fast, my face getting warm and my stomach knotting up. I'm sure my reaction would have been suspicious to another adult but my four-year old didn't seem to notice. The man who had been my husband was going to marry again and Lisa was going to be my son's stepmother.

Lisa, the other woman, had been around since Ian and I had separated the year before. We had had some interaction with one another but communication was mainly with Ian, which was still tense and not easy. Today, I faced this new revelation. The divorce still hurt. I still felt unsettled being a single woman and mother. How was I going to accept this new fact?

After their marriage, Lisa was establishing her role as their family matriarch, and more times than not it rubbed me the wrong way. She had a certain way of doing things and I had my way of doing things and we were asking Cole to be adaptable to both which I felt was unfair to Cole. I felt threatened as Cole's "real" mother. Time and time again, our conversations dissolved into "she said/ he said" scenarios. I was feeling I had to give up my "dreams" of how I wanted motherhood to look and it scared me.

After a heated discussion with Ian and Lisa, I remember getting down on my knees while the tears streamed down my face and cried to God, "Why did this have to be so hard?" "Why did I feel like the enemy when Ian was the one who wanted out?" "Why did we question everything with each other when we both knew we had similar value systems?" "Why did he trust her opinion over mine?"

I prayed for strength and above all, for wisdom. After I was spent, totally exhausted venting these questions to God, I began asking, "What did I want for Cole?" "Did I want him to see an angry mother?" "Did I want him to feel like he had to pick sides?" "How did I want him to see his parents communicate with each other?" I knew that Lisa and I communicated much better than Ian and I did. She didn't have the deep-grooved recordings that Ian and I had established over the years. She heard me differently than he did. She heard me as a mother and a woman, not necessarily as Ian's ex-wife.

My ultimate desire was for Cole to see a parenting relationship that was respectful, cooperative and supportive to his wellbeing so he could feel loved by all of us—and that included Lisa. Lisa's nature genuinely seemed to care for Cole. She was teaching him, holding him accountable and loving him. At the time, she didn't have kids of her own, and I saw that her expectations were high. Lisa established a home for Cole where he had two other sets of loving grandparents. I asked myself, "Wasn't that a good thing?" I had to make a choice. I asked God to heal me, to teach me to forgive and for wisdom to see this situation differently. Proverbs 3:5-6 became my mantra: "Trust in God with all my heart and do not lean on my own understanding. In all my ways acknowledge Him and He will make my path straight."

We connected as mothers at a deeper understanding of the sacrifices mothers give innately because they love their kids.

As I released control of how the relationship "had" to look, the more I saw a beautiful relationship forming between Cole and Lisa. It was happening without sacrificing my relationship with Cole. Both could develop simultaneously. Our parenting unit was moving forward, smoother than before. It was still a little sticky and sometimes stalled on the muddy trail. In time, Lisa and I began to trust one another, whether we agreed or not. We really tried to listen—staying on the topic at hand. I remember a conversation we had after she had her twins. She was extremely fatigued as she was establishing a schedule for them. Our conversation was getting heated and my voice started cracking. She asked, "Are you crying?" "Yes," I said. "Why?" she wondered. "I remember how tired I was when Cole was first born and from one mother to another, I think you are amazing. I can't imagine how fatigued you are as a mother of twins. You seem to be holding it together so well." At that moment, we connected as mothers not as Lisa and Michele, with our individual agendas, but at a deeper understanding of the sacrifices mothers give innately because they love their kids.

Today, I can say that I <u>participate</u> in a working parental relationship and it contains three people—all raising OUR son. Cole is loved by a big family that contains one father and two mothers, and a large extended family. He trusts that we are united in looking after his wellbeing. The three of us collaborate using our unique gifts to foster his growth as a young man.

The other woman was not the enemy. Instead, God helped me see Lisa as a blessing in Cole's upbringing. I'm grateful that Lisa accepted the role as stepmom and that she battled her way through the journey with me, along with God's grace, to get where we are today.

To learn more about Michele de Reus, visit www.expertauthorpublishing.com/cob.

True Financial Freedom
Bob Burnham

When I was 17, I loaned my dad money from the investment company I ran with some friends. My dad took a long time to pay us back, which really worried me. Stress over financial issues was a defining factor in my early life and for years afterward.

Despite my knack for making it, money has been the source of a lot of fear, anger and anxiety for me most of my life. Being wrapped up in these intense emotions has affected all my personal relationships, including those with my family growing up, my marital relationship, and my relationships with my children.

As a very young kid, I felt our family was well off and secure, living in a nice middle-class home. I remember vividly how spectacular cartoons looked on our color TV, the first in the neighborhood and a big deal. My dad had a busy TV repair business with a full-time employee and we had two new cars parked in the garage.

When I was 10, my dad's TV repair business started to fail and money became a very real issue for our family. That feeling of comfort and having everything I needed disappeared just like a carpet being pulled out from under my feet.

I recall balancing on the edge of my seat in anticipation as I waited for my dad to return from his rich uncle's house, asking to borrow money. If his uncle said yes, it would help our family survive a few months longer. He did bail us out several times. What a sense of relief if my dad returned with good news.

As the TV repair business struggled, Mom and Dad did many things to survive with the money they had. There was a bigger mortgage on the house, then a second mortgage at high interest. My dad would still talk about getting rich and buying a new Lincoln, but deep down I felt angry about the whole situation. The financial security I had once taken for granted was gone.

In hindsight, my upbringing was a mixed blessing. Anxiety about money became a main focus for me and affected me for decades. But ultimately, these challenges put me on the path to true financial freedom and a sense of peace and clarity in my everyday life.

My ability to organize and make money became obvious early on. At 12, I was the kid with a bunch of paper routes around the neighborhood and a staff to deliver them. My earnings let me buy my own drum kit when I was 13. At 17, the investment company I had with several friends financed the purchases of most of my neighborhood friends' cars.

I became a successful businessman and was working a lot. The problem was, no matter where I was or what I was doing, I thought I should be somewhere else.

If I was driving to a location to visit a customer, I would think, "I shouldn't be doing this! My time would be better spent at the office catching up on paperwork."

If I was at the office doing paperwork, I would be preoccupied with the thought, "Maybe I should be out supervising workers." It was hard to concentrate with this endless worrying.

By my late 20s, my carpet cleaning company was doing over six million dollars in sales per year. With that kind of income, I assumed that a feeling of financial security would follow, but having more money only made me feel I had less and less money. I was so infused with self-doubt, I could barely think, and I felt fearful I would lose the money I had. Then what would I do? Already an angry person, I became angrier.

Watching the world increased my sense of insecurity. The stock market could crash, a real estate bubble might burst, what looked like a solid investment could be revealed as a ponzi scheme. I worried that similar uncertainties would affect my wealth.

As time went on, obstacles kept coming up in my business. I felt I had to keep scrambling to make more money. I thought, "as soon as these problems are out of the way, I'll be able to enjoy life."

I sought help from books, seminars, coaches and mentors. Finally, the change happened when I stopped struggling so hard against each and every negative emotion, allowing me to take a step back; and, instead of seeing just trees, a new sense of distance allowed me to see the whole forest at once. A couple of deep realizations came to me. Number One: My knack for making money is part of my makeup and something I can count on. Number Two: When you take negative emotions out of the mix and replace them with peace of mind you can see all of the possibilities around you. I was sitting in front of my computer. I felt so incredibly changed on the inside that I wondered how I could still be the same person on the outside. I may still look the same, but I've felt and thought differently ever since! For example, I had been doing public speaking for some time. I had the idea that I wanted to write, publish and sell my information. Almost immediately there was a possibility of purchasing a small publishing company. Later, a writer I knew contacted me out of the blue. Then, it happened that a current associate was also interesting in publishing. It seemed that all of the building blocks for this new business were falling right into my lap! I may not have seen all of this as an opportunity a few years before. Now, my broader view and my faith in my own business sense have allowed me to develop the idea, and it has absolutely taken off. It's an amazing feeling!

Treat problems as blessings and they will help you move forward in business and in life.

Life is full of problems, and I realize that I will always have them—but treat problems as blessings and they will help you move forward in business and in life. By doing this, I have found true financial security. I understand now it comes from within me, a combination of the knack I've had for making money since I was a kid and my ability to see the overall picture clearly. Strip away everything, put me in an unfamiliar situation, and within the hour I'd figure a way to make some money out of it. This security in my own financial abundance is something no one can steal from me.

I think back to the days when I'd be driving one way and thinking I should be headed in the opposite direction. Or when I'd be scrambling to make money. Or when I was nervous, ticked off, scared, or all three! I've had everything I've ever wanted all along, but I wasn't aware of it. I see the big picture clearly now. I am able to be much more present in the moment. I don't need to be anywhere else when I sit down to dinner with my family. I am able to savor the food and the company. I know I have true financial security and I can provide for them. I am grateful.

To learn more about Bob Burnham, visit www.expertauthorpublishing.com/cob.

Love Unexpected
Monica Regan

I had been walking a blistering 25 kilometers a day on the Camino de Santiago for about three weeks when I was blindsided by the man who would teach me more about love than I had ever known. The Camino is a pilgrim's route some 800 kilometers across Spain, filled with seekers of every kind, and I was on it to connect with myself. I loved my self-chosen solitude, my simple life out of my backpack, my trusty walking stick and the growing sense of peace within me as I walked each day through valleys and villages in the golden sun. Everything I read about the Camino had suggested that everyone has a love affair on the road, but I was determined to be alone. If I was going to have a love affair, it was going to be with myself, and as far as I was concerned other pilgrims were a distraction from that.

It seems the Camino had other plans for me. After three weeks of avoiding other pilgrims, I awoke in the biggest hostel I had come across. The hostel breakfast of *café con leche* and bread awaited me in a crowded eating area and I was forced to share a table with a group of pilgrims who, it seemed, had met the night before whilst partying in town. To my distaste, one of them leaned over and began to speak to me as if I had been a part of their shenanigans. The lines around his inky-black eyes crinkled in laughter when I explained that I was not part of their group. He apologized for his mistake and wished me a *buen camino*.

After a few hours back on the Camino, I managed to find myself lost, but to my dismay, with the same group from breakfast. I was going to have to talk to them and so I participated in much map consulting and head scratching until we were back on route and at a crossroads where the Camino split. Pleased for the opportunity to escape, I announced I would take the other path to the group but then the inky-eyed man from earlier announced he would join me. To my own surprise, I approved of his declaration. We shook hands in greeting and headed down the dusty path together.

As we walked, I learned that he was Basque, married and very entertaining. By the time we reached the next hostel, we had shared so many laughs that my stomach ached, as well as so many personal vulnerabilities that we had both been moved to tears. There was an undeniable chemistry between us but as he was married, I dared not let myself think of him romantically.

Over the next week we were inseparable. We ate, meandered, meditated, drank beer, laughed and talked incessantly together and our friendship reached a level of intimacy that I had not known before with anyone. Deny it as I tried, I was besotted. And it was the cleanest and most profound connection I had ever experienced. I admired his integrity and fidelity, as we both knew that there was something powerful happening between us. We kept the boundaries and his conscience clear; he spoke to his wife regularly and had told her about the connection he felt to me. She gave him freedom, but he knew that even though we had something very special, it wasn't meant to be and we all knew he would return to her.

When the end of the Camino was but a few days walk farther, I began to feel the pain of knowing I would be separated from this man that I had learned so much from about love, vulnerability, trust, integrity and laughter. This thought caused me agony. I was clinging onto those precious days and desperate for our powerful connection to continue on.

The thought of losing him pained me so much that I found it hard to continue at his side. I avoided him and walked with a Dutch student that I had met in a hostel. This student gave me his ear while I recounted our relationship, expressing my increasing sense of dread over parting ways with this man. Patient and wise, my young Dutch friend said something to me that changed everything. He said,

"Monica, you cannot lose what has already been. Nothing lasts, but nothing is lost either. Everything only changes."

I could choose to be full of gratitude for what I had, not grief for what I was losing.

And in a moment I saw that I was suffering because of my attachment to the idea that I could only be happy if I could maintain the magnificent connection I had with my Basque love: that in losing him, I was losing everything. But what that young Dutch boy said allowed me to realize that what I had had was a gift. My experience was not changed because it was ending, it was simply evolving into something else. The love I felt, everything I had shared and learned, they were still mine and they had been blessings. My attachment to having it continue was stealing from the richness of what had been. Letting go of this attachment gave me the freedom to feel how lucky and blessed I had been to have had the experience at all. Instantly, it is was clear that I could choose to be full of gratitude for what I had, not grief for what I was losing; our last few hours together could be filled with joy, not pain.

So the Camino did have a love affair in store for me. But it wasn't the kind of love affair I expected. I said goodbye to the Basque man and we stayed friends through the magic of the Internet. My Camino love affair taught me that nothing lasts, but nothing is lost either, everything only changes. And that changed everything for me. Now I appreciate my blessings while they are with me, and when it is time to let them go I create space for something new to evolve.

To learn more about Monica Regan, visit
www.expertauthorpublishing.com/cob.

The Tools

Self-Soothing
Healing From the Inside Out
Tammi Baliszewski, Ph. D.

Many of us have heard this term in regard to babies and toddlers. But I have found in order to become a spiritually mature adult, we need to change our beliefs about the way we are being treated and learn to soothe ourselves on the mental, emotional and spiritual levels. Self-soothing techniques are things you can do for yourself to make yourself feel better in any situation. They are completely self-contained and do not rely upon the input, opinion or contribution of others. This makes them both powerful and empowering.

If you rely on the good opinion of others to make you feel okay about yourself, this gives them an enormous amount of power over you. They have the option and power to withhold what you want or need, which can put you in a vulnerable, precarious and victim-like position. By developing your own methods for self-soothing, you are able to care for yourself in positive, powerful and proactive ways. When you learn to implement self-soothing techniques you naturally and easily become more whole, complete, balanced, stable, and healthy in body, mind and spirit.

Anytime we are in emotional distress, and especially if it is out of proportion for what is actually happening, it is because of something unhealed within ourselves. For example, one day while washing dishes I chipped a chunk of purple porcelain off of a dinner plate. My husband Steve witnessed this and scowled at me sternly. I looked at him, confused, and said with indignation (and possibly louder than I needed to): *"What's your problem?"* He responded angrily, saying: *"Can't we keep anything nice around here?"* His expression, words and tone cut me to the quick. I put the plate back into the soapy water, dropped the sponge and stomped out of the kitchen.

    I was feeling really upset, so I checked in with the part of me that was hurting. I asked inwardly who needed my attention, and what came forward was a younger part of myself, she seemed about 8 years old. I asked her how she was doing. She said: "Not too well." I asked her what she needed, and she let me know that she needed to be acknowledged for trying to be helpful and that she needed to be loved. So I took responsibility for her/me, and told myself what I needed to hear. I told my inner eight year old Steve was going through his own stuff and it wasn't personal. Then I told her I thought she was doing a great job and I loved her. The hurt lifted and I immediately felt better.

    My husband came in a few minutes later still fuming. But now because I was on solid emotional ground within myself, I could have a clear conversation with him without making him wrong or the bad guy. I asked him what was going on. He told me it bothered him that I chipped the plate. I told him it seemed to me there was something more going on than a four-dollar chipped plate. I asked what was beneath his upset; what was really going on? He stopped and thought for a minute.

Then he told me he was frustrated by some things going on at work, his employees were not listening to him. Then he apologized, saying it really didn't have anything to do with the plate, or me. If I had not taken the time to self-soothe, this predicament could have escalated and continued on for some time, possibly ruining our entire weekend.

I invite friends, students and clients to implement this self-soothing technique as well, and they often experience miraculous results. I had a client, Kathy, who was having problems with her older brother. His actions and words were causing her great pain. I had her go inward and check in: Who was hurting? She said an image of herself as a teenager came forward. I asked her what she was feeling. She said she was sad because her big brother didn't like her. I asked her what she needed, she said she needed to be seen and loved. So then I had Kathy bring her own attention and love to her inner teenager. She did so, and by the end of the appointment, said she felt much better. She left me a message the following day, saying something really ironic had happened. When I called her back, she told me earlier that morning her brother called, and without her saying a thing, apologized for not being more available to her. Then he invited her to lunch to spend some "quality sibling time together." She was stunned, yet grateful. She asked me if I thought this was weird. I told her no, I did not think this was weird at all. I witness miracles just like this all the time after doing the self-soothing inner work in my own life and in my practice.

Why does self-soothing work? Because outer reality is a reflection of inner reality. So, as we learn to take responsibility for our inner reality, our outer reality naturally shifts and transforms. Another way to look at this is to realize if something is causing us upset or pain, the upset or pain is not outside of us, it is inside of us. Healing occurs when we bring attention, compassion and love to the places inside that hurt. No one else can do this for us—even though we may really want them to! I have often thought if my husband is nice to me, then I will feel better. No, what I need to do is find a way to feel better, then my husband is nice to me!

Choosing to feel better is choosing to take responsibility for ourselves. This is an empowered stance that serves us in all areas of our lives.

I had another friend, Marion, who was dealing with a frustrating pattern. She was working a lot but having problems collecting payment for the jobs she had completed. I had her go inside and ask who needed her attention. She said a 14 year old showed up. I asked her what she decided about herself and about life at 14. She said she learned that she needed to be quiet and good. Her sisters and brothers were always fighting and causing her mother a great deal of stress. I asked her inner 14 year old what she needed to hear. She said she needed to hear that she had value and her thoughts and opinions mattered. I invited Marion to tell her inner 14 year old those things. Marion asked if I would do it for her and I said no, this work only works when WE take responsibility for OURSELVES.

The goal is not to look outside of ourselves for love, attention and validation, but to attend to, love and validate ourselves. And so Marion said what the younger version of her longed to hear and found that she felt better immediately. The next day a check arrived in the mail for a job she had completed over a month ago. Then she received a call from another client who was in the neighborhood and wanted to drop her money off to her. A third payment showed up two days later. Coincidence? I don't think so. Synchronistic and miraculous? Absolutely!

Often when we are hurting we look for surrogates to heal ourselves. Often a person who has unhealed trauma looks for another who is hurting and believes if he or she can fix or heal that person, it will somehow help them. This is usually an unconscious belief that rules our lives from the shadows. Then there is the other dynamic where we are convinced if we get what we need from that other person we will be fixed and healed. People who are hurting attract other people who are hurting, it is called "parallel wounds." It is like a merry-go-round that goes round and round but never gets anywhere. Self-soothing is the tool that helps us get off the merry-go-round and supports us in creating happier, more stable and more fulfilling lives.

Exercise for self-soothing:
1. Consider an unpleasant reoccurring pattern in your life, or a situation where you were recently hurt or upset.

2. Now turn inward and ask yourself, "Who inside of me is hurting right now?" and invite that younger part of yourself to come forward. Do not have an attachment to what happens next. It may be an aspect of yourself at any age or time in your life, from an infant, to teenager, to adult.
3. Ask them how they are doing and how they are feeling. Listen inwardly to whatever they have to say.
4. Ask them what they need from you now to feel better.
5. Ask them what they yearn to hear.
6. Now, share the words and messages that this inner one longs to hear.

This is a simple exercise that can support you in locating the solid ground within and can serve you for the rest of your life. When you are more stable, healthy and whole, you attract and are attracted to more stable, healthy and whole people. Drama decreases and synchronicity increases. Discernment and intuition are also up-leveled and refined. And as you continue to self-soothe and inwardly validate the worth and value of your "inner selves," you will find your worth and value being reflected back to you in amazing ways— both financially and in relationships.

We have often heard, "Treat others the way you want to be treated," which is wonderful wisdom, but I think to go to the next level of fulfillment in our lives, we need to treat ourselves the way we want to be treated. Listen to, attend to and honor yourself. Nurture yourself, be loving, kind and generous with yourself. And, as you do, you will find the world shifts and transforms around you in exquisite, beautiful and miraculous ways!

To learn more about Tammi Baliszewski, Ph.D., visit www.expertauthorpublishing.com/cob.

How To Identify Your Subconscious Beliefs in Minutes
Nikkea B. Devida

I. BACKGROUND

Process of Manifestation

B →T →F →A = R

Beliefs → **Thoughts** → **Feelings** → **Actions** = **Results**

Your **Beliefs** lead to your **Thoughts** lead to your **Feelings** lead to your **Actions** = Your **Results**

When you change your beliefs, you change your results. If you're not satisfied with the results you're getting, you probably have *subconscious* beliefs that are not in alignment with your results.

Definitions
- **Perception:** Awareness of the environment through physical sensation.
- **Beliefs:** Beliefs are conclusions, derived from perceptions, information and/or experiences. Beliefs can be both conscious and subconscious. Subconscious beliefs drive behavior and results far more than conscious beliefs.

How Subconscious Beliefs Are Formed
- By taking in information through our five senses: Visual, Auditory, Kinesthetic, Gustatory, and Olfactory (VAKGO). This information is stored in the subconscious mind.
- Sensory Experiences (VAKGO) X Repetition = Subconscious Beliefs
- Subconscious Beliefs + Experiences X Repetition = Habits
- Habits cause automatic perceptions and behavior = RESULTS
- Your actions create the results in your life but are NOT the cause.

Subconscious Beliefs Are Filters for Reality
- You See the World NOT As It Is ... **But As YOU Are!**
- Subconscious beliefs create perceptions that affect every area of your life. These subconscious beliefs act as filters and get in the way of truth and possibilities. You don't see the world as it is, you actually see the world as you believe and perceive it to be.
- Your inner human software is the accumulation of your subconscious beliefs, which control what you can do. These subconscious beliefs can be self supporting or self limiting.
- These subconscious beliefs drive behaviors— which lead to and create your results!

- Subconscious beliefs are neural patterns that are stored in the brain. The more a neuron is fired, the stronger the impulse gets and the easier it is to go down that neural pathway.
- Thoughts are biochemical, electrical impulses. **Translation: Thoughts are REAL things!**
- Your mind is a programmable bio-computer. According to Dr Bruce Lipton, *your mind is not analogous to a computer chip, it is homologous to a computer chip.*
- **Translation: Your mind is not LIKE a computer chip ... it IS a computer chip!**
- Inner conflicts and conditioning (our behaviors) are held in place by patterns of energy and information, held in the subconscious mind. Beliefs that created the conditioning are just photons of light held in an electromagnetic field. To change our behavior, it is most efficient and effective to change the beliefs held in the subconscious mind. This directly changes the field—the photons of light, to create a new field. Changing the document (beliefs) directly in the computer (subconscious mind) changes the photons of light held in an electromagnetic field.

II. CONSCIOUS/SUBCONSCIOUS/ SUPERCONSCIOUS MIND

The missing link between good intentions and effective action is the alignment of subconscious beliefs with conscious goals. The missing link between achieving goals and actual fulfillment is the alignment of the conscious goals with the superconscious mind. ACT™ aligns all three levels of the mind.

Conscious Mind
- This is the part of you that thinks and reasons. Your free will lies here. This is the part of your mind that will decide the changes required to live the type of life you want to experience. The conscious mind can accept or reject any idea.
- Conscious impulses travel at 120-140 MPH and the conscious mind has a processing capacity of 2,000 bits of information per second.
- Functions of Conscious Mind are memory, reasoning, will, and imagination. This is the part of you that sets goals and evaluates your results.

Subconscious Mind
- The subconscious mind expresses itself through you in thoughts, feelings and actions. Your experiences over time get impressed upon the subconscious and become fixed in this part of your personality. Fixed ideas will then continue to express themselves without any conscious assistance. It has no ability to reject and no filters. This is especially true before the age of 5, and to some extent before age 12. Fixed ideas are more commonly referred to as habits and the collective habits are referred to as the "conditioned mind."

This is the part of you that is habitual, automatic, and "programmed" based on this conditioning.
- Subconscious impulses travel at more than 100,000 MPH and the subconscious mind has a processing capacity of over **4 Billion** bits of information per second.
- Functions of Subconscious Mind are to store beliefs, memories, and habits; it is your personal operating system. Everything you've ever seen, heard or experienced is stored in your subconscious mind. The subconscious mind functions in every cell of your body.

Superconscious Mind
- The superconscious mind is frequently referred to as the spiritual side of your personality or the universal mind. The superconscious mind knows no limits, except for those you consciously choose.
- Function of Superconscious Mind is to connect you to the source of all supply; the Universal Infinite Intelligence.

We manifest most powerfully when we have our subconscious, conscious and superconscious minds in full alignment with each other. When that exists, we are able to accomplish anything that we choose that is in our highest and best good.

III. OVERALL GOALS VS. BELIEF STATEMENTS

Think of your Overall Goal as your destination, and the individual Belief Statements are all the different highways, streets, and roads that you need to take to arrive at your destination. Having the right beliefs in your subconscious supports you in achieving your goals

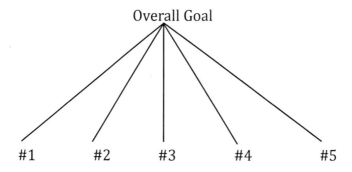

Belief Statements—#1 to #5, etc.

How To Create Well-Formed Belief Statements for the Subconscious Mind:
 a. **In the first person.** It is most powerful when you are personally connected to and involved with the statement. These are most commonly "I" statements.
 b. **In the present tense.** The subconscious is present time only. Therefore, belief statements in the present are most powerful. These are most commonly "I am ..." statements. For example, "I am happy" is more powerful than "I will be happy" or

"I am going to be happy". We cannot test for the future. All the muscle test tells us is what is true in this moment. This is why it is not useful, and in fact can be misleading, to try to use kinesiology for predicting things or making decisions in the future.

c. **A statement rather than a question.** We use statements rather than questions because we are not trying to get yes or no answers to questions. We are getting indications that there is a resonance or there is not a resonance with what is being presented to the system.

d. **Stated in the positive, as if it's already true.** Make the belief statements in the positive. This may feel like the "big lie" right now. Perfect. Once the belief statement is aligned, this creates a powerful <u>dynamic tension</u> between your inner reality and your outer reality. The subconscious mind (4 billion bit processor) will be working to draw this new reality to you so that the inner and outer realities are congruent.

Our subconscious tends to filter out the words "no" or "not". For example, let's say you currently don't have enough clients or money and you're in in a pattern of attracting potential clients who have no money and can't pay for your services. If you would like to attract better clients, then "I have a full practice of #_____ full paying ideal clients" may be a good belief statement to use.

Avoid a statement such as "I no longer attract clients who can't pay for my services".
e. **Create your own belief statements.** Use the worksheet on the next page to create your own belief statements. Also refer to the Sample Belief Statements for additional ideas.

Overall Goals & Belief Statements Worksheet

A. **Identify the Problem:** What's the problem? How are things now?

B. **Identify the Solution:** What is the "opposite" of the problem? If you didn't have that problem, what or how would life be like instead? What would you have instead? How do you want things to be?

OVERALL GOAL:_____

_____

_____

_____

C. **Brainstorming:** What would need to be true in order for you to achieve your goal? What would you need to believe about yourself in order to achieve your goal? What would you need to believe about others, your "environment", the Universe/God, etc. for you to achieve your goal?

D. **Create Belief Statements:** Turn the previous statements of desire from B and C into first person, present tense belief statements.

E. **Intention Check:** Remember, every goal may have both an "up" side and a "down" side. Are there any potential negative consequences to achieving this goal for yourself or others? Is that okay with you and do you still choose to proceed with this goal?

IV. HOW TO COMMUNICATE DIRECTLY WITH YOUR SUBCONSCIOUS MIND

What Is Muscle Testing? A Biofeedback Testing Technique

Muscle testing is also called kinesiology or muscle checking. These terms are interchangeable and synonymous. Kinesiology is the scientific study of the body's movements and is a method of getting useful information from the body/mind/emotional system. With its proper use, we can present something to the system and then see if there is alignment or congruence between what we present and what is inside of our body/mind/emotional system. It is the practice of testing or checking the muscle's response to different kinds of stimuli.

Muscle testing is an easy and effective method of detecting the presence or absence of stress (i.e. inner conflict) in the body/mind/emotional system. It also establishes a convenient "yes/no" communication system with the subconscious mind and can be an accurate detector of subconscious beliefs.

Muscle testing is the main method to communicate with your subconscious mind used in the Accelerated Change Template (ACT)™ Belief Change System. You will learn how to muscle test yourself using a variety of methods. Our primary goal with muscle testing is to identify and change subconscious beliefs.

How Does Muscle Testing Work?
An easy and effective way to communicate with the Subconscious Mind is with Muscle Testing, <u>because</u> the subconscious controls motor functions such as muscle movement.
- Muscle Testing is a communication link with the Subconscious Mind
- Subconscious Mind controls the Autonomic Nervous System
- Autonomic Nervous System controls Muscle Movement/Viscera
- Brain sends Electrical Signals via the Autonomic Nervous System
- Strength of Electrical Signal determines Muscle Response
- Presence or Absence of Stress affects Electrical Signal Strength
  - *Increase Stress →Decrease Muscle Strength
  - *Decrease Stress → Increase Muscle Strength
- Muscle Testing allows us to observe/perceive Stress via Signal Strength via Muscle Strength

<u>Sources of Stress</u>
- Conflict—Subconscious Beliefs
- Emotional
- Physical

When Stress is present, the Muscle Test is weak due to decreased Electrical Signal Strength.

When you are not congruent with a subconscious belief, you will test weak to it.

When you are congruent with a subconscious belief, you will test strong to it.

Instructions to Identify Your Subconscious Beliefs

Refer to the video for this program to see the demonstration of how to directly communicate with your subconscious mind with **Self Muscle Testing** and a demonstration of **Self Muscle Testing Methods** (pages 214-218).

To view the video, go to www.expertauthorpublishing.com/cob.

Once you reach my website, enter your First Name, Last Name, and Primary Email in the online form to receive the video and other free gifts.

Then, muscle test yourself for each of the Belief Statements you created from the **Overall Goals & Belief Statements Worksheet** (pages 209-210), and the **Sample Belief Statements** (page 219-220) on the **Belief Statements Worksheet** (page 221-222).

Self Muscle Testing

There are many methods to use for self muscle testing. The following is a list of the more commonly used self muscle testing methods. Although it is not a complete list, you will probably find at least one method that works for you. Try several of them and practice with them until you feel proficient enough to do alignments on your own. You only need to be proficient with one to identify your subconscious beliefs and facilitate your own alignments to change those beliefs.

The list below suggests what the signals may be for a "yes" and "no" response.

Remember, YOU get to decide what represents "yes" or "no" based on your calibration step. With any or all of the methods below, your signals may be different. Go with your own signal based on your own calibration step.

The key is to practice, practice, practice!!!!

I recommend that you practice each method for 1-2 minutes to see if that method works for you. Remember, you only need one that works reliably for you. If you get reliable signals with more than one, just keep using the one you like the best.

CALIBRATE— Identify your own "yes" signal and your "no" signal. Do this with each self muscle testing method used, as well as <u>each time</u> you use it because your signals may change each time.
- Muscle Test:*"Please show me a 'yes.'"* Notice the response.
- Muscle Test:*"Please show me a 'no.'"* Notice the response.

Important Note: To get the most reliable muscle testing signals, maintain a "neutral", "curious" and "open" attitude about whether a particular muscle test will be STRONG/ON or WEAK/OFF.

Self Muscle Testing Methods

Find A Self Muscle Testing Method That Works Best For You

1. **Pendulum**
   When you say to the pendulum, "Please show me a yes/no," the pendulum will begin to swing in a particular pattern. You probably have a natural direction for "yes" and "no". It may be clockwise, counterclockwise, back and forth, diagonal, standing still, etc.
   CALIBRATE—Muscle Test: *"Please show me a yes/no."* Notice the response.
2. **Finger-Pinch**
   Gently pinch your right thumb and first finger together, enclose them in a similar left-handed pinch. Ask your calibration questions and try to open your right pinch against the left one.
   CALIBRATE—Muscle Test: *"Please show me a yes/no."* Notice the response.
3. **Double Pinch Chain**
   Put one pinch inside the other like two links of a chain. Ask your calibration questions and try to pull them apart.

CALIBRATE—Muscle Test: *"Please show me a yes/no."* Notice the response.

NOTE: You only need to find one self-muscle testing method that works reliably for you.

How to Use Self Muscle Testing

The first step with any of the self muscle testing methods is to "calibrate." That simply means that you need to know what your own "yes" signal is and what your "no" signal is. The following Communication step can be used for self muscle testing. Remain open, neutral, and curious!

STEP 1: SET UP COMMUNICATION WITH YOUR SUBCONSCIOUS MIND:

A. **CALIBRATE**—Identify your own "yes" signal and your "no" signal. Do this with each self muscle testing method used, as well as <u>each time</u> you use it because your signals may change each time.
- Muscle Test: *"Please show me a 'yes'."* Notice the response.
- Muscle Test: *"Please show me a 'no'."* Notice the response.

B. **LIKE/DISLIKE**—Stress Detector
- <u>Silently</u> think of and get into the feeling of something you like.
- Self Muscle Test

- **Silently** think of and get into the feeling of something you dislike.
- Self Muscle Test

C. **TRUE/FALSE**—Detector of Subconscious Truths
- Say <u>out loud</u> something that is obviously true about yourself, and get into the feeling of the true statement as you say it.

Examples: *"My name is Sarah/Jim." "I am a woman/man." "I am an engineer/secretary."*
- Self Muscle Test
- Say <u>out loud</u> something that is obviously false about yourself, and get into the feeling of the false statement as you say it.
- Self Muscle Test

D. **YES/NO**—Communication System
- Repeat the word "*YES*" over and over.
- Be <u>neutral</u> while saying yes.
- Self Muscle Test
- Repeat the word "*NO*" over and over.
- Be <u>neutral</u> while saying no.
- Self Muscle Test

Don't proceed until you have established clear, solid communication!

How to Identify Beliefs in the Subconscious Mind

Use your "yes" and "no" responses/signals from the calibration in Step 1 (or muscle test with a partner). Say belief statement out loud and muscle test.

MUSCLE TEST BELIEF STATEMENT

Muscle Test: The desired Belief Statement
- Say the desired belief statement <u>out loud</u> as you get into the feeling and emotion of the belief statement.
- Examples: See also Sample Beliefs Statements worksheet
  "I deserve to live the life of my dreams."
  "I am at peace with my body and I love my body just the way it is."
  "Money flows to me easily and I always have all that I need."
  Say "***Clear Signal***" and Muscle Test

If WEAK: You are not congruent or in alignment with that belief in your subconscious mind. You can use the ACT™ Belief Change System to change that belief and install it directly into your subconscious mind. (www.acceleratedchangetemplate.com)
If STRONG: Congratulations! You are already congruent with that belief in your subconscious mind and are able to maintain a whole brain state with respect to that

belief. There's nothing you need to do. That belief is already operating in your subconscious mind.

NOTE: Muscle testing belief statements is very similar to the True/False test in Step 1C when you Set Up Communication with your subconscious mind.

TRUE/FALSE—Detector of Subconscious Truths
- Have your partner say <u>out loud</u> something that is obviously true/false about them and get into the feeling of the true/false statement as you say it.
- Examples: *"My name is Sarah/Jim."*
  "I am a woman/man."
  "I am a coach/mechanical engineer."
  "I am 5'4"/12'9."
- Say "***Clear Signal***" and Muscle Test

Sample Belief Statements
1. I now earn $_____ per year in my career/business doing work that I love and living a lifestyle I love.
2. I now earn $_____ per year while working _____ days/hrs per week, and taking _____ weeks vacation per year.
3. Money flows to me easily and I always have all that I need.
4. I make a lot of money and I now have a lifestyle and a life that I love, with the time, resources, vitality, and loving relationships to enjoy it.
5. I have the power to create my life just the way I want it.
6. It's okay for change, life and success to be easy for me.
7. The best of everything comes to me and I easily attract and manifest that which is in my highest and best good for myself and others.
8. I now manifest the _____ (home, relationship, business, health, etc.) of my dreams.
9. I set goals and achieve them easily and confidently.
10. I deserve the very best in life and life is easy for me.
11. I deserve to live the life of my dreams.
12. I am energetic and full of health and vitality.
13. I can eat whatever I want and easily maintain my ideal weight of _____ lbs.

14. I take care of my physical needs (sleep, eating, sex, etc.) in healthy, positive ways that delight me.
15. It is easy for me to do what it takes to maintain a thin, healthy, fit body.
16. It's easy for me to maintain my ideal weight of _____ pounds.
17. I am comfortable in my own skin.
18. I am at peace with my body and I love my body just the way it is.
19. I now have my ideal body.
20. I now enjoy a loving, fun, committed, romantic relationship with the man/woman of my dreams.
21. I am worthy of a happy, long lasting relationship with the man/woman of my dreams.
22. It's safe for me to give and receive love.
23. I am safe in the world.
24. It is safe for me to trust myself and others in my life.
25. I love and accept myself as I am and as I change.

Belief Statement Worksheet

Column A:

Conscious Mind: Rate yourself with regard to each of the 25 Belief Statements as it relates to how it is in your life now. 1= 100% Disagreement up to 10= 100% Agreement

Column B:

Subconscious Mind: Muscle test each of the Belief Statements. Note response in column B. STRONG = "+" and WEAK = "-"

Column A   Column B   Column C

1. _____ _____   _____
2. _____ _____   _____
3. _____ _____   _____
4. _____ _____   _____
5. _____ _____   _____
6. _____ _____   _____
7. _____ _____   _____
8. _____ _____   _____
9. _____ _____   _____
10. _____ _____   _____
11. _____ _____   _____
12. _____ _____   _____
13. _____ _____   _____
14. _____ _____   _____
15. _____ _____   _____
16. _____ _____   _____
17. _____ _____   _____

18. _____ _____   _____
19. _____ _____   _____
20. _____ _____   _____
21. _____ _____   _____
22. _____ _____   _____
23. _____ _____   _____
24. _____ _____   _____
25. _____ _____   _____

Column C:
What did you learn or notice? Any patterns? Any surprises?

©2011 Peregrine InSight Group, LLC. Printed with permission.

For more information on Nikkea Devida, visit expertauthorpublishing.com/cob

DISCLAIMER: The following tool offers rapid, lasting subconscious changes in beliefs and emotional patterns. Working alone on issues of intense trauma, without benefit of a health provider or counselor, is not recommended. Neither is this simple, powerful tool advised for witnesses in lawsuits where emotional state of mind is at issue, prior to trial, without the consent of your lawyer.

A Tool to Achieve Instant Breakthroughs to Your Ideal Results in Any Situation
Kit Furey, JD, CHT, CEHP

What's in this tool for you? What do you prefer in your favorite "transformational tools"? When you want to make lasting changes in your experiences and results, are you like me in that you want simplicity in a process? And elegance? A tool that is powerful and effective? That delivers easy, gentle, lasting results? Do you want at your disposal a tool that, once it's in place, almost runs on "autopilot" to unlock limiting subconscious patterns? What if all you have to do is simply focus your awareness on your "other than optimum" experience (that is, on your thoughts, emotions and body sensations), choose to move toward more inner freedom, then send a specific signal to your subconscious to do all the heavy lifting to clear out the subconscious patterns that are creating your problematic experience? Tools with those qualities are the ones I love most! And that is precisely the kind of tool I'm sharing with you now.

Complex practices, protocols and tools get shelved in my world, even if they deliver what they promise. Why is that? Because there's zero requirement that life be hard or cumbersome. And because changing limiting beliefs and emotional patterns can be simple, when you have the right "know how" and the right tool. In fact, I've made a comprehensive study of a multitude of transformational tools. I'm delighted to share one simple, powerful, easy-to-apply tool that delivers profound and consistent results when you want to dissolve the root causes of limiting beliefs and emotional upsets.

Once you put the tool in place by giving your subconscious a one-time instruction that's presented in this article, you're all set. After that you simply notice when you're having an experience you'd rather not be having, intend to change your experience, and put your subconscious to work by thinking or saying your "cue".

We'll put the pieces of this tool together bit by bit so you can create **instant breakthroughs** *out of* **"other than optimum experiences" and** *into what you want instead.* What do you want? More peace, freedom, joy, love? You choose! Dissolve what's stopping you and open up to attracting and creating what you want instead. Do it now, with ease and grace!

Here's why your beliefs are either good news ... or not: Research in the field of neuroscience demonstrates that about 95 to 99% of the results you experience in your life are driven by beliefs you hold in your subconscious (rather than your conscious) mind. So conscious choice counts, to be sure, yet your real power comes from what's going on in your subconscious. If what you consciously choose is aligned with what is actually programmed in your subconscious, you achieve effortless results. If your conscious choices and subconscious beliefs and programs are out of alignment, though, if they aren't congruent, then you experience inner tension and have difficulty achieving the results you want. **So what's critical is what you really believe, rather than what you think you believe. Think about that a moment, why don't you?**

For our purposes, **a belief is a statement you think is true or correct, whether you are conscious of it or not.** I'm reminded of a story about how one family's recipe for cooking a ham required cutting off both ends of the ham. The daughter asked her mother why that was. The mother wasn't sure "why," only that "it's just how to cook a ham." But the daughter asked her grandmother about the recipe, and the grandmother said, "Oh, that's because the only pan I had wasn't large enough to hold a full ham. So I had to make the ham fit the pan." The daughter questioned the belief about how to cook a ham and discovered the **belief was limiting and ripe for an update.** In the model I use when I'm working with clients, I use 3 broad categories of core limiting beliefs: Abandonment and Betrayal; Significance and Self-Worth; and Trust, Safety, Surrender, Discernment. In just a moment I'm going to demonstrate how I dissolved a belief of mine about "Significance and Self-Worth." Most people have a limiting belief or two in this category! Perhaps you do, too.

Without going into deep detail about how we form beliefs (a comprehensive special report is available on my website for those of you who are curious about how we humans are wired, and who want a thumbnail sketch of functional distinctions among levels of mind,) just know there's ample scientific research to support this statement: Humans are neurologically "wired" to make meaning of experience. It has to do with the mammalian brain. You see, hear, feel, sense, taste, smell and from that sensory experience the brain generates thoughts about the experience, from which conclusions are made, thus forming beliefs; and those patterns of beliefs drive emotions and behavior. And the beliefs that drive emotions and behavior can propel you toward your highest potential. Or lock you in limbo. And limiting beliefs keep you at odds with your True Self (also known by some as your Higher Consciousness or Soul or Being or your I AM Presence), at odds with what you know on your deepest levels is possible for you.

When what you believe to be true is consistent, congruent, aligned on all your levels of mind (including your Being,) your life flows with ease, grace, and harmony. However, when you hold a subconscious belief that is at odds and somehow limits the fullest expression of your Being, that limitation will become evident to you in some way—directly (e.g. you experience something that isn't what you want and you recognize the pattern or result as being the product of a limiting belief) or indirectly (e.g. something is amiss in your life, "other than optimum," and you're baffled to understand what's going on.) That invisible, baffling, "something that's going on" is undoubtedly the result of a limiting subconscious belief.

And the good news about self-limiting beliefs is that so long as you have

1. an abiding trust that since you created or unconsciously accepted (think about the mother who chopped off the ends of the ham) any limiting beliefs you have, you can therefore change and update ones that don't work for you anymore, and
2. a heart-felt desire to Be your full potential, and
3. a commitment to yourself to consistently apply effective belief change tools until you have unshackled yourself from beliefs that aren't moving you toward Being your full potential,

then the world is your oyster. Period. So clear out or update the beliefs and emotional patterns that limit you, that create the "other than optimum experiences" in your life. Open up your oyster and free yourself to Be. Allow your life to flow with ease, grace and harmony. And just know that the change process can be easy, gentle, rapid and lasting. You can create Instant Breakthroughs.

Now **Let's Put the Tool in Place for You**: Next I'm going to share a method (or tool) from a modality called

Be Set Free Fast(TM) (BSFF), developed by clinical psychologist Dr. Larry P. Nims. There are thousands of BSFF practitioners worldwide, and I'm honored to be one of 10 internationally authorized instructors of this method. And I love to share BSFF with people because it's simple, easy to learn and it works every time.

The method will work for all varieties of limiting beliefs, emotions or patterns of perception. And lest you think I'm going to approach this simply as a "talking head," rest assured I'll be using an acute experience in my own life to illustrate how to apply each and every step of this tool. **My example is going to illustrate applying the tool in the context of "Relationships" to a belief about my "Significance and Self-Worth."**

Remember that the tool applies regardless of context (e.g., Money and Abundance, stress that affects Health & Well-Being, or your Spiritual Awakening, just for starters.) And in fact, I chose "Significance and Self-Worth" as the core limiting belief example because it almost always affects every category of core limiting belief and plays out in every aspect of people's lives. Give some thought now to how your beliefs about your Significance and Self-Worth might be limiting you right now.

Think about "money and abundance" for example. Your beliefs about your significance, what you deserve, your sense of self-worth, are mirrored in the cash flow of your life. Not enough money in your life? I'll bet money there's some sort of lurking limiting belief about deserving to have lots of money. So if "money" is what's up on the radar of your life, this tool's for you!

As I lay out how to put this tool in place, I encourage to "work along with me" and apply the tool to something you'd like to shift in your life. That way you get to unlock and dissolve some of your inner baggage as your read along. And achieving results will be easy, gentle, rapid and lasting. Fair enough? Here we go.

My story about bumping into a limiting belief about Significance and Self-Worth: Once upon a time I got a call from my aunt wondering if my children and I would like to ride with her to the wedding reception of my brother. Very thoughtful invitation. Except that my children and I hadn't been invited to either the wedding or the reception. The shock of this incident registered as "traumatic" on my inner Richter Scale, resulting in time spent in the fetal position wrapped up in my quilt. If I were inclined to suck my thumb, that's when it would have happened. This shock was that bad. And within a few weeks my pulse was so high I thought I was in the Big Checkout Line of Life. Medication required. And, savvy belief and energy transformation expert that I am, my question to myself became, "What belief do I have that is creating such a reaction in me?" What I uncovered, with persistence and great diligence, was a belief about "not deserving all manner of good things." And the kicker was it wasn't just my belief about me ... the further I dived in, the further back up the family tree the energy of the limiting pattern persisted. (Generation upon generation of "cutting the ends off the ham.") Naturally, I set about shifting the belief ... for me as well as shifting the energy at levels of higher consciousness in the whole family system.

(How to shift beliefs on behalf of your entire soul lineage and biological family is beyond the scope of this article; however, with some advanced "know how" regarding the use of this tool, you can send healing beams of love that offer transformation beyond the bounds of time and space. That's so important in this day and age, in my opinion!)

My story goes on. Fast forward from several years to about a year ago. I've been diligently putting a new business model in place. Working long hours and working very hard, in fact. It's been exciting, and absorbing all the new information has been quite challenging. I called my 90-year old father to wish him a happy birthday and I asked what he'd done that day. His response? "Absolutely nothing of consequence. Probably just like what you do in a day." In the moment I concluded the comment was intentionally hurtful and rude, and I brought the phone call to a conclusion. Then came a flood of tears. And it is at this point in the "once upon a time" that we will begin to apply the steps of the tool I'm excited to share with you. Because you see, I'm going to show you how I've changed the belief that caused my tears, created my upset, sparked my "other than optimum experience." And you can do this for anything you're experiencing that isn't optimum, too! Money and Abundance. Relationships. Health and Well-Being. Spiritual Awakening. Big stuff or small stuff.

So let's get to the nitty gritty and put this amazing tool in place in your repertoire of self-help tools, shall we?

Step 1 (a) Notice your experience and (b) "calibrate or assess" your experience (your thoughts, emotions, physical sensations.)

Step 1(a.) Notice your experience. Does whatever you're experiencing feel good? Are your thoughts and inner dialogue uplifting and empowering? Or are you criticizing yourself or making yourself wrong? Or, God forbid, wondering "Am I good enough?" (I say this because you may be in the habit of just muscling through anything and everything in order to maintain your momentum. Ignoring what doesn't feel good or seems dis-empowering? Stuffing it, perhaps?) **With this tool, though, you don't have to tolerate any experience that's "other than optimum" ever again.** With this tool you can now shift everything you want to. Truly. Stay with me here. We're putting the building blocks of the tool in place. And it **starts with being attuned to what you're actually experiencing.** Notice what's going on with you, and notice if it feels good, or not.

Step 1 (b.) Calibrate your experience. Is what you're experiencing "Good"? Or could your experience be better? If it could be better, in other words if your experience is "other than optimum," then calibrate—like taking your temperature—to see how much better your experience could be in order for it to be your ideal experience.

Here's one way to calibrate your experience: on a scale of 0-12, 12 being your divine ideal and 0 being your worst nightmare, far worse than you ever have or ever will experience, simply ask, "On a scale of 0-12, where is this experience for me now?" You'll become aware of a number, and you can jot that number down so you can compare how much you've changed by the end of this exercise.

My example: Step 1—(a) Notice experience and (b) calibrate/ assess your experience: I'm on the phone with my dad. He makes a comment that seems odd and critical of me. In the moment, my inner dialogue is "I don't like how that comment feels. Ok. I'm finished with my birthday wish. Going to hang up now. This is not ok with me." **(b) Calibrate: "Where am I now regarding this upset, 0-12?"** Then I just allow myself to become aware of a number. And if I think I'm not getting a number, I ask, "And if I had become aware of a number, what is that number?" Then I jot that number down so I can track my progress. (Just FYI, my calibration for this experience is a 6 and 12 on this 0-12 scale would be ideally "free from upset". So I notice there's an opportunity for me to dissolve some patterns that are creating hurt feelings in me.)

Now it's your turn: Step 1— (a) Notice your experience(s) (your thoughts, emotions, physical sensations) and choose a specific experience that's "other than optimum" for purposes of shifting the underlying beliefs and emotional patterns that created your experience. **(b) Calibrate or assess your experience** by asking, "0-12, 12 being my divine ideal experience, free of any upset, where is this experience for me now?" Write down the number you become aware of so you can notice what's changed for you by the end of this exercise. As much as anything, this step lets your conscious mind know something happened, even though your conscious mind doesn't need to "understand" anything for this tool to work.

Step 2. Set Intent to Dissolve the Limiting Subconscious Pattern(s). If your experience is "other than optimum," then you get to choose whether to shift toward a better experience or not. If you choose to shift toward a better experience, set Intent to change the pattern. For our purposes, "Intent" is simply a conscious choice to achieve a particular outcome.

My example: Step 2—Intent. As I hung up the phone with my dad I was thinking, "Well, I stayed pretty neutral while I was on the phone. But now I'm feeling hurt. That comment seemed intentionally unkind. And feeling hurt is simply not a way I want to expend my energy. So I choose to shift whatever it is in me that makes me feel hurt."

Now it's your turn: Step 2—Intent. You've noticed your "other than optimum" experience; you've calibrated your experience; now you intend to do something about the patterns that are creating your 'other than optimum' experience. It's simple. Just consciously choose when you think or say: "I intend to change this pattern/belief/experience." Write down your intent now so you can track your belief changes:

Step 3. (a) Give a One Time Instruction to Your Subconscious About What You Want it to do When You Use Your Cue, and (b) Putting it all Together: Notice, Intend, Use the Cue Until You Feel Complete. Because the subconscious mind is literal and consistently and predictably does what it is programmed to do (and there are different ways to program the subconscious; however, describing those various methods is outside the scope of this article,) you can consciously direct the subconscious.

We're going to do that now, giving your subconscious an abbreviated one-time instruction from Be Set Free Fast (BSFF), developed by clinical psychologist Dr. Larry Nims. In addition to being a clinical psychologist, he's trained in NLP, EFT and Thought Field Therapy. So you get a lot of benefits when you're using the BSFF modality. **You only have to give this abbreviated instruction to your subconscious one time.** BSFF is amazing in its simplicity and effectiveness. You can use this tool any time, anywhere and no one will be any the wiser or have an inkling that you're taking charge of your experience right then and there.

Step 3 (a)—Give a One Time Instruction to Your Subconscious About What You Want it to do When You Use Your Cue This next building block gives your subconscious a one-time instruction about what your subconscious is to do each and every time you notice your experience, intend to dissolve limiting subconscious patterns, and you direct your subconscious to get to work by thinking or saying your cue. (May I recommend you choose the cue, "All Clear"?)

Here's the abbreviated instruction. (This instruction will be like taking a 30 mile an hour test drive of a tool that will take you 120 miles an hour when you give your subconscious the comprehensive set of instructions, which are way too comprehensive to include in this article.) Again, you only have to give the instruction to your subconscious this one time. After that, your subconscious will just follow the instructions whenever you intend to shift your experience and use your cue. How does it get any better than this?)

"I'm accessing, from the morphic field, the instructions and definitions of Be Set Free Fast in this quick BSFF version. When I'm speaking like this I am talking to you, subconscious, in all the dimensions and all the energy systems you connect to. Whenever I say or think the words, "All Clear," you will dissolve any thought, feeling, emotion, memory, fantasy, sensation, problem, issue, need to act or react, or anything else I notice on any level that causes me harm or distress or confusion. You will do this immediately, permanently and faithfully, back to the original roots of what you are dissolving."

If this instruction is acceptable to you, think or say "All Clear" to confirm this to your subconscious now.

That's it. Your Be Set Free Fast cue is now in place, and it functions like a light switch, flipping your subconscious into gear to dissolve the root causes of self-limiting patterns. All you have to consciously do is notice your experience, intend to dissolve the patterns creating your "other than optimum" experience, and direct your subconscious to go to work when you think or say your "All Clear" cue. (Intent is essential. If you say or hear the words "All Clear" in casual conversation, this tool doesn't activate. Your subconscious goes goes to work to follow the instruction only when you intentionally direct it to by using the All Clear signal.)

Step 3 (b)—Putting it all Together: Notice, Intend, Use the Cue Until You Feel Complete.

My example: Step 3—Putting it all Together to Dissolve the Root Causes of "Other Than Optimum Experiences:" Notice, Intend, Cue. I'm off the phone, I feel upset, I've calibrated my experience as a 6 on a 0-12 scale, and I'm choosing (setting intent) to dissolve the patterns that are the root cause of me feeling upset.

Now what I do is just "stay in my experience" and begin to shift the root causes of my experience by **using the cue for everything I notice: thoughts, emotions, limiting beliefs I become aware of, everything that's "other than optimum."** I do this until I feel a sense of completion, or I'm at the end of the time I have available for "doing my inner transformational work." I can always pick up where I left off at a later time if I haven't reached a sense of completion. So here's how it went

for me ... notice as you read through what I experienced that I intended and signaled my subconscious to dissolve a variety of thoughts, emotions, body sensations. Notice, too, that my thoughts, emotions and body sensations did not emerge in any particular order:
- I feel astonished by the remark (in my solar plexus area). All Clear
- I feel a heaviness ... All Clear ... Sadness ... All Clear ... "less than" in my heart All Clear
- I'm thinking, "I don't deserve to be treated that way!" All Clear and then "Why can't he see that I do important work?" All Clear "It's always like this." All Clear "Some things are never going to change." All Clear "I'm really finished with this dance we do. Totally finished." All Clear
- Still feeling heaviness in my heart. All Clear
- Tears. All Clear
- This is just how it is with us. All Clear
- I really don't like how this feels. All Clear
- I don't like it when anyone says what I do is insignificant. All Clear
- I think my work is significant. All Clear
- I AM significant. All Clear
- What other people think of me is none of my business. All Clear
- His comment hurts. All Clear
- I really have zero idea what he could be thinking that would prompt a comment like that. All Clear
- I choose to dissolve every thought, feeling, attitude, belief, imagination and every other problem

- that I have ever had about or toward wanting my dad's approval. All Clear
- I choose to dissolve every thought, feeling, attitude, belief, imagination and every other problem that I have ever had as a result of wanting my dad's approval. All Clear.
- I'm feeling calm now. All Clear
- I really am the only one who has the power to decide if what I do is significant. All Clear
- And I wouldn't do what I do if my Soul weren't calling me to do what I do. All Clear
- And the bottom line is that if I'm okay with me and choose to believe what I do is significant, and that I AM significant, that is enough. All Clear
- In fact, I think I'll just forgive my dad for what he said. All Clear
- For whatever he meant by what he said. All Clear
- And for whatever meaning I made of his remark that caused me to feel hurt. All Clear
- I forgive myself for feeling hurt. All Clear
- And know that everyone does the best they can, including Dad and me. All Clear
- And I choose to dissolve all anger, judgment and criticism of myself. All Clear
- And I choose to dissolve all unforgiveness toward myself. All Clear

Now it's your Turn: Step 3—Putting it all Together to Dissolve the Root Causes of "Other Than Optimum Experiences:" Notice, Intend, Cue.

Notice: What are you experiencing (or you did experience) that's "other than optimum"? Thoughts, emotions, body sensations, etc.
Calibrate/ Assess Your Upset: "0-12, 12 being my ideal, free of upset, Where is this experience for me now? You'll become aware of a number. Jot that down if you wish so you can track your shifts. (Your conscious mind will like this.)
Choose to shift your experience or not. If you want to change your patterns of experience, simply set intent to do so. For example: "I want to change this experience." Next, you simply stay in your experience and use your cue to dissolve whatever it is you notice you're experiencing.

Then you simply think or say "All Clear" to signal to your subconscious that you want it to follow the instruction you gave it to dissolve the root causes of the patterns that are creating your "other than optimum experience." (Remember, it's only necessary to give the instruction one time because the subconscious is literal and consistent in doing what it's programmed to do.) Just stay in your experience, noticing your thoughts, emotions and physical sensations, and use your All Clear cue for everything you're experiencing.

Step 4. Notice What's Changed and Recalibrate Your Experience.
My example: Step 4—Re-Calibrate. Ok. I've noticed the details of my experience ... my emotions,

my thoughts and I've used my All Clear cue until I reached a sense of calm and completion. I simply ask myself again, "0-12,12 being my ideal experience, free of limitation, where am I now?" And notice what's changed. When I'm at a 12, then I know that I've dissolved the relevant patterns for this experience. If, when I re-calibrate, I'm at less than 12, I can either just continue to notice my experience, and I can also ask my subconscious: "What would it serve me to know or do now in order to move from ___(calibration) to a 12?" Then I just wait until my subconscious offers a signal or response in the form of a thought, emotion or physical sensation. When that happens, I simply follow my experience and use All Clear for everything I notice. Using this tool is really that simple.

In my example, I'm now at a 12 for the flare up of the limiting belief about my significance. Whew! My dad is about to have another birthday, and I'm curious to notice my experience and **Notice** if I'm now creating a more pleasant experience for myself. I **calibrate my upset** if I'm not. And direct my subconscious to go after more layers of limiting beliefs and emotions when I **use the All Clear cue** if I'm experiencing something that's "other than optimum." Because if my experience is "other than optimum," it's simply a problem that this Be Set Free Fast tool can dissolve. How does it get any better than that?

Now it's your turn: Step 4—Re-calibrate to notice what's changed. Simply ask yourself again, "0-12, 12 being my ideal experience, free of limitation, where am I now?" And notice what's changed when you compare this number with the number you noticed when you started this exercise.

Here are Some Answers to Frequently Asked Questions About Using this BSFF Tool:

1. **Do I have the full power of this tool available to me now?** Actually, this exercise and abbreviated instruction give you an experience of how the tool works. And the abbreviated instruction is just that: a 30 mile an hour test drive of an amazing tool that will take you 120 miles per hour (at least!) when you give the one-time comprehensive set of instructions to your subconscious.
2. **What if I notice I'm having an "other than optimum experience," (e.g. maybe I'm distracted and I want to focus on something important and just can't seem to zero in on what I'm doing) but I don't know why I'm distracted (or upset?)** The good news is you don't have to know why you're experiencing what you are. Your subconscious knows what beliefs and emotional patterns are linked to your current experience, and when you intend to shift those patterns and use your "All Clear" cue, the subconscious follows the instruction you gave it and dissolves those patterns. This tool is simple, yet powerful and creates lasting results.

3. **What if I don't think anything has changed?** Your subconscious will faithfully follow the instruction you gave it, each and every time you intend to dissolve the limiting patterns and think or say your All Clear cue. Think of your limiting patterns as if they were an iceberg. With each use of your Cue, your subconscious shaves off a layer of the iceberg that is your cluster of limiting beliefs and patterns. Every time. Whether your conscious mind is aware of the shift or not. And to calm the conscious mind's concern about whether something happened, I teach people how to do the 0-12 pre and post calibrations. It helps the conscious mind "get" that something "real" happened. Know that your subconscious has dissolved at least a layer of the iceberg that represents the root causes of your problem if you intended it to!
4. **What if I don't feel any physical sensations when I'm using my All Clear cue?** That's ok. Some people do experience physical sensations when they are shifting, like changes in body temperature, buzzing in their ears, or a feeling of momentary pressure in their head or somewhere in their body, or a feeling like something "just released." Whatever you experienced is just right for you, including feeling nothing at all. And calibrating helps your conscious mind "know" the magnitude of the change you just experienced.

5. **How can I learn more about this Be Set Free Fast tool?** There's information available at expertauthorpublishing.com/cob

And when you want to discover how the full power of this extraordinary tool can help you unlock and dissolve patterns of limitation in your world, please go to my website and complete an application for a complimentary Instant Breakthrough Discovery Session. At my website I'd love to guide you to discover your greatest obstacle to achieving your ideal results in Money & Abundance, Relationships, Health & Well-Being and Spiritual Awakening.

For more information on Kit Furey, visit expertauthorpublishing.com/cob.

Meta Belief Change Technique
Irena O'Brien, Ph.D., ACMC

The first thing that you need to do to change a belief is to identify its structure. I had two beliefs that were causing me problems: 1. That I had to be perfect. 2. Because I wasn't perfect, I would be rejected. I tried to change those beliefs separately, and although I knew at an intellectual level that they didn't make sense, the thought of making a mistake or being in social situations where I could be rejected still triggered a fight-or-flight response. What made a big difference for me was the "Meta-Stating Concepts" technique developed by L. Michael Hall. This was so transformational for me that I eventually became an Associate Certified Meta-Coach (ACMC).

Before we get into the details of the technique, it's important to understand how we create beliefs. As human beings, we have an incredible ability to take our experiences of the outside world and give them meaning (the term "meaning" is synonymous with the word "belief"). In fact, we attach meaning to all of our experiences, that's how we make sense of the world. We are also reflexive beings in that we have thoughts and feelings, and then thoughts and feelings about those thoughts and feelings, and thoughts and feelings about those thoughts and feelings, and so on. **Consequently, our meanings are layered upon each other and our ultimate meaning may no longer look anything like our original experience.** These first, deeply-rooted "higher-level meanings" tend to drop out of our consciousness, so we are no longer aware of them even though they guide our behavior.

We also don't think linearly, but rather our mind meanders and coils back on itself, creating loops and spirals. These loops can either serve us or they can be destructive: They can form vicious circles that keep us stuck and pull us downward, or positive loops that propel us forward, toward our excellence.

In my case, my originating experience was my time in the hospital at 2 years of age. The meaning I attached to the experience was that my parents had abandoned me because I wasn't good enough. Thereafter, my life was about trying to be perfect, and I constantly watched myself for potential mistakes to try to curtail them before they happened. I also avoided people so that they wouldn't reject me. But I didn't see the loop I was in. I wasn't able to see how I had built up meaning upon meaning to form a loop. And I was stuck inside that loop, going round and round and round.

Our meanings or perceptions can be positive and enhance our lives, or dangerous and destructive. Our meanings become part of our map of the world through which we deal with people and events. They become a code by which we organize our lives, and they act as filters through which we perceive the world, and through which we attract experiences that confirm the meanings we've attached to events, consciously or subconsciously. I was attracting experiences that highlighted my mistakes. I was also attracting rejection. I saw rejection everywhere and approached people hesitantly. When meeting someone new, I looked for evidence of rejection. My definition was very broad. I defined rejection as not being openly welcoming; if they weren't openly welcoming, I would interpret that as rejection and walk away. No wonder people didn't warm up to me immediately—I was rejecting them first! So we need to be careful about which meanings we choose. Toxic meanings will give us toxic lives. It is the meanings we assign to our experience, not our experiences themselves, that create our reality.

In summary, we make meanings at many levels. The purpose of the following technique is to uncover our levels of meaning, our belief map about a concept or idea that we live by. The higher up the levels we go (into early core meanings), the less aware we are of our beliefs. This technique will help you discover those higher-level beliefs that you're not aware of. By going up the levels, you will discover a loop if you have one. In any event, even if you're not in a loop, with this technique you will discover your higher-level meanings that may not be working for you, or that may be toxic. This technique also gives you the formula for changing those toxic higher-level beliefs. For example, although generosity is a positive concept to live by, it becomes unhealthy when we need to be generous at all costs, when we need to sacrifice ourselves. Some major examples of concepts that we may have difficulty with are: money, relationships, time, power, rejection, failure, sexuality and trust.

Technique:

This technique looks difficult but is in fact quite simple. It will take you deep into the levels of meanings to uncover the belief map that governs your actions and your life. I have included a concrete example further on to guide you.

- Identify a concept that gives you problems. The following questions can help you identify what that is:
- What concept do you want to develop a better relationship with?
- What concept, idea, or understanding pushes your buttons?
- Complete the sentence stem: "I have a problem with ..." (authority, dependency, women, intimacy, entitlement, freedom, morality, vulnerability, criticism, fairness, failure, etc.)
- What comes to mind when you finish the sentence stem: "I can't stand ..."

Most likely you have more than one concept you may want to explore, but you'll get the ultimate freedom by working with the concept that causes you the most problems. How do you know which one that is? If there's a concept that keeps coming up again and again, or one you absolutely do not want to touch, that's the one!

- Explore the meaning levels and belief map about the concept. Start by asking and answering questions about the concept. Use the question that works for you (if one of the questions doesn't produce an answer, try another). At the first level, keep asking what else do you believe about your concept until there are no more answers. Then pick one first level belief and start asking questions about that belief, and if you get an answer, that's it for that level. Then go up the levels by asking questions about the previous meaning.

1. What do you believe about _____?
2. What does _____ mean to you?
3. When you think about _____ what other thoughts come to mind?

Always ask the question about the previous meaning that came up. Keep track of the layers by writing down your answers, and keep asking the questions about the previous meaning until there are no more layers (no more answers). Ignore answers that are feelings or emotions, or that are actions. They are not meanings. Otherwise, don't censor your answers. Usually, the first thought that comes to mind, no matter how wacky or unlikely, is the right answer. Also watch out for answers that repeat the previous meaning using different words. These are not really different meanings but a repetition of the previous meaning. For example, if you are examining vulnerability and the thought that comes up is *"I could open myself up to being taken advantage of,"* you are simply repeating the same thing using different words. Keep going up the levels until you have no more answers. Then take another first level belief and do the same thing (you may discover that you have more higher level beliefs that you weren't aware of).

Have you discovered that you're in a loop?
What triggers or sets up the idea or concept?
When does this concept or idea come up? What specific event triggers it? Describe the event or situation fully. You only need to work with one situation here. Make sure that this is what comes up immediately before the cascade of meanings start. It could be a thought, an image in your mind, a feeling, or something that you hear or see.

Note: If it is difficult to come up with meanings in step 2, do step 3 first. But remember, finding the meanings in step 2 may take some effort. You do have them. You just need to uncover them.

4. So this is what triggers the idea or concept; when you see, hear, or feel this, then the concept arises automatically?

Do you need this concept as you have mapped it?
Does it enhance your life and empower you, or is it limiting or toxic?

5. Build up a new, empowering set of meanings about the trigger.

Ask yourself: What else could this trigger mean? Could it mean something else? Develop a new, better meaning for the trigger. Then ask: If the trigger has this new meaning, what would that mean? And then what would that mean? etc. Build upon it.

To illustrate how this technique works, here is an example of the belief map I uncovered using this technique, and the new belief map I built up.

Step 1:
The concept that I had a problem with was perfectionism.

Step 2:
Q: What do you believe about perfectionism?
A: *That I have to be perfect.*
Q: What else do you believe about perfectionism?
A: *There's nothing else. I have to be perfect.*
[Here, I only had one first level belief so I didn't need to repeat this step]
Q: So what do you believe about having to be perfect?
A: *If I'm not perfect, I'm flawed*
Q: What do you believe about being flawed?
A: *If I'm flawed then I'm worthless*
Q: What do you believe about being worthless?
A: *If I'm worthless, then I'll be rejected*
Q: What do you believe about being rejected?
A: *If I'm rejected, then that proves that I'm worthless.*
(Here is the loop: worthless → rejected → proves I'm worthless)

Step 3:
Q: What is the trigger that sets off this set of meanings? How does the cascade of meanings start? You only need to work with one situation here. The trigger could be a look from someone. What else could that look mean? How do you know you're interpreting this look correctly? How do you know what that person means by the look?
A: *When I have to meet someone I don't know, I freeze and all I can think about is not being perfect and them not liking me. I'm so afraid of saying something wrong, it feels like a lump in my chest that I can't get past.*

Step 4:
Q: What else could that "freezing" and that lump in your chest mean?
A: *It's always meant that I have to run away. But I guess it's normal for people to feel some anxiety before they meet someone new. So I could redefine it as normal anxiety about meeting new people; that it takes 2 people to have a conversation so if it doesn't go well, that doesn't mean I wasn't okay. They just might not be interested in meeting me. In fact, it probably has nothing to do with me.*

Step 5:
Q: If that's true, what would you need to believe about that?
A: *I would need to believe that it's not all my fault if it doesn't go well.*

Q: And what would you need to believe about it not being your fault if it doesn't go well?
A: That I'm not flawed.
Q: What would you need to believe about not being flawed?
A: That I'm not worthless; that I have value, that I'm okay the way I am.
Q: And what would you need to believe about having value?
A: That they may not be interested in talking to me for a variety of reasons that have nothing to do with whether I'm perfect or not.
Q: Now, how do you feel about perfectionism and rejection?
A: I feel much more relaxed about approaching people; just because a conversation doesn't go well doesn't mean that it has to be my fault; that perfectionism is a concept I don't want to live with any longer.
Q: Do you need to keep perfectionism in your life any longer and have it run your life?
A: No, I don't. I don't need perfectionism anymore
Q: Are you sure, or do you want to keep it and have it control your life for another 5 or 10 years?
A: Yes, I'm sure. I don't want it anymore.
Q: Now create your new belief—what else could the trigger mean in a positive way? Etc.

To illustrate how this technique works, I've mapped out both my old belief map and my new belief map below. (Read from bottom up.)

My Old Belief Map

Trigger: I freeze when I have to meet new people

The trigger caused the cascade of beliefs that got me stuck in the loop. Until I identified my belief map, I was not aware that I was in a loop. That's why my previous efforts at working with perfectionism and rejection separately were only partially successful.

Here is how I mapped out my new beliefs. Notice that there is no loop here.

My New Belief Map

I have value; I'm okay

I don't have to be perfect to be okay

I'm not flawed

It's not solely my fault if it doesn't go well

It's normal to feel some anxiety when meeting new people

Trigger: I freeze when I have to meet new people

In my new belief map, there is no loop. When I do experience the trigger, the old fight-or-flight response wants to kick in. When I consciously redefine it as "it's normal to have some anxiety when meeting new people," the new belief map rather than the old belief map gets activated.

In this example, the overarching belief is that I'm worthless. Even with something simple, such as trying to lose some weight, I'd tell myself that going on a diet meant I was flawed. "I'm worthless if I need to go on a diet," would lead to "I'm not going on a diet because I don't want to feel worthless." When people get stuck, they often tell themselves, "What good does it do to (go on a diet, exercise etc.), they often don't want to admit that they have feelings of worthlessness or hopelessness because they are terrified of sinking into a mire of feelings they have no clue how to address because they don't even remember how they got them. Then they are stuck with this belief, "If I'm not even willing to go on a diet, that must prove I'm worthless too."

Since I discovered my core meaning that "I'm worthless," I've been following my Weight Watchers and I don't feel like cheating. I've been incredibly successful in losing weight.

People think they make conscious decisions but often they are run by very old programs starting from birth to age 5 that they have no memory of.

I have found that if anyone is stuck and never seem to get past procrastination, have an inability to find lasting love, or make just enough money to get by, there must be some belief that's stopping them. And, just like me, they'll find a multitude of areas that will be transformed in their lives once they change that belief.

For more information on Irena O'Brien, visit expertauthorpublishing.com/cob

Information on Contributing Authors

For information on the writers that contributed stories and provided Belief Change Tools, please visit expertauthorpublishing.com/cob.

CPSIA information can be obtained at www.ICGtesting.com
Printed in the USA
LVOW071607310812

296892LV00022B/63/P